Ken Kesey

Twayne's United States Authors Series

Warren French, Editor

Indiana University, Indianapolis

TUSAS 444

KEN KESEY
(1935–   )
Photograph reprinted by permission of Faye Kesey

Ken Kesey

By Stephen L. Tanner

Brigham Young University

Twayne Publishers • Boston

Ken Kesey

Stephen L. Tanner

Copyright © 1983 by G.K. Hall & Company
All Rights Reserved
Published by Twayne Publishers
A Division of G. K. Hall & Company
70 Lincoln Street
Boston, Massachusetts 02111

Book Production by Marne B. Sultz

Book Design by Barbara Anderson

Printed on permanent/durable acid-free
paper and bound in the United States of
America.

Library of Congress Cataloging in Publication Data

Tanner, Stephen L.
  Ken Kesey.

  (Twayne's United States authors series;
  TUSAS 444)
  Bibliography: p. 150
  Includes index.
  1. Kesey, Ken—Criticism and interpretation.
I. Title. II. Series.
PS3561.E667Z88   1983   813'.54   82-18717
ISBN 0-8057-7383-5

For Madlyn

Contents

About the Author

Stephen L. Tanner received the B.A. and M.A. degrees from the University of Utah. After receiving the Ph.D. from the University of Wisconsin in 1969, he joined the English faculty at the University of Idaho. He was a Senior Fulbright Lecturer in Brazil during 1974–1976 and in Portugal during 1979. Currently he is Professor of English at Brigham Young University. He has published widely in such periodicals as *American Literature, Shakespeare Quarterly, Studies in Romanticism, Essays in Literature, English Language Notes,* and *Southwest Review.* He recently completed a book on Paul Elmer More. In addition to courses in American literature, he teaches literary criticism. Much of his time outside the classroom and library is spent hunting and fishing.

Preface

Does the author of just two novels warrant a book-length study? Much depends upon the two novels. In Kesey's case they are clearly significant. *One Flew Over the Cuckoo's Nest* has been both a remarkable best seller and an unusually popular literature text. In fact, it has frequently been used for courses besides those in literature. The amount of criticism and commentary it has provoked demonstrates its impact during the last twenty years. *Sometimes a Great Notion* is significant in quite a different way. Although it has not enjoyed the wide popularity and recognition of *Cuckoo's Nest,* it is a major novel in its scope and technical innovation and accomplishment. In the long term it may prove to be more important than *Cuckoo's Nest.*

Besides being the author of these novels, Kesey is the subject of a widely read book by Tom Wolfe: *The Electric Kool-Aid Acid Test.* This book, a notable literary achievement itself, chronicles his activities as a leader in the California psychedelic revolution that transformed the Beats into the hippies. His career helps us understand the nature and consequences of that movement and the larger cultural trends of which it was a part.

From the standpoint of cultural and literary phenomena, Kesey is of special interest because his career displays a blending of nineteenth-century rural and twentieth-century urban elements. On the one hand, his writing displays the characteristics of frontier humor and oral tales and expresses the frontier values of self reliance, independence, and physical strength. On the other, his writing and other activities manifest the attitudes and behavior of urban radical culture. He embodies impulses and tensions important in shaping American culture during the third quarter of the twentieth century: the impulse to return to nature in the face of manipulative technology; the impulse to seek altered states of consciousness in the face of overwhelming materialism; the tension between nostalgia for the values and myths of the western frontier experience and rejection of the past in favor of radical social-cultural change. To examine Kesey's career is to gain an illuminating view of a generation's attempt to alter American consciousness.

In addition, Kesey provides an interesting test case for the possible creative stimulus of hallucinogenic drugs. He seriously and energetically experimented with psychedelic chemicals in an attempt to open new doors of perception and expression. The results provide valuable information concerning the relationship between chemicals and creativity.

He is also significant as an instance of a talented writer attempting to go beyond writing to new forms of expression. After two successful novels, he turned away from writing in search of expression transcending the written word. His quest instructs us concerning the vital and enduring importance of language in artistic expression.

Thus he warrants attention not only as an exceptional (although not prolific) novelist but as a leader in a cultural movement and an explorer in the realm of drugs and creativity. As Tony Tanner points out in *City of Words: American Fiction 1950–1970,* "for anyone interested in trying to appreciate what was going on in both American literature and society in the late sixties, Kesey is a figure who has to be understood and, it seems to me, respected."[1]

I have given most attention to his novels but have also tried to analyze and evaluate his nonliterary or semiliterary activities. I have not tried to cover the same ground Tom Wolfe did; this seemed unnecessary. Instead, I have addressed questions raised by his book and attempted from our present perspective to determine the achievements and consequences of Kesey's psychedelic investigations and escapades.

I have made use of the Kesey Collection at the University of Oregon Library, several boxes of manuscripts, letters, notes, and tapes. Quotations from letters, notes, and other unpublished material are from this collection and are generally not footnoted. Excerpts from this material have been published in *Kesey,* edited by Michael Strelow and the staff of the *Northwest Review*; I have noted when the material I quote appears in that book. In quoting from the unpublished material, I have silently corrected obvious misspellings.

Stephen L. Tanner

Brigham Young University

Acknowledgments

I am grateful to Brigham Young University for two summer research fellowships and to the editors of *Southwest Review* for allowing me to use material that first appeared in their pages.

I also want to thank the following people for their help and cooperation: Ken and Faye Kesey; Ken's mother, Mrs. Ed Jolley; and Kenneth W. Ducket, Curator of Special Collections at the University of Oregon Library.

Chronology

1935   Ken Elton Kesey born La Junta, Colorado, 17 September.

1946   Family moves to Springfield, Oregon.

1956   Marries Faye Haxby.

1957   Graduates from University of Oregon.

1958   "End of Autumn" (unpublished novel).

1959   Enters creative writing program at Stanford on a Woodrow Wilson Fellowship.

1961   Volunteers for government drug experiments and works as psychiatric aide at Menlo Park VA Hospital. "Zoo" (unpublished novel).

1962   *One Flew Over the Cuckoo's Nest.*

1963   Stage version of *Cuckoo's Nest.*

1964   *Sometimes a Great Notion.* Cross-country bus trip with the Merry Pranksters filming "The Movie."

1965   Arrested in April for possession of marijuana.

1966   Arrested in January for possession of marijuana. Flees to Mexico. Returns in late fall and is arrested.

1967   Convicted and spends June to November in the San Mateo County Jail and later at the San Mateo County Sheriff's Honor Camp.

1968   Moves to Pleasant Hill, Oregon. Tom Wolfe's *The Electric Kool-Aid Acid Test.*

1969   Lives in London from March to June, doing some work for *Apple.*

1971   Coedits (with Paul Krassner) *The Last Supplement to the Whole Earth Catalog.*

1973   *Kesey's Garage Sale.*

1974   *Spit in the Ocean,* no. 1, including "The Thrice-Thrown Tranny-Man or Orgy at Palo Alto High School" and the first part of *Seven Prayers by Grandma Whittier.* Travels to Egypt in search of the Secret Pyramid and publishes dispatches in *Rolling Stone.*

1976   *Spit in the Ocean,* no. 2, including second part of *Seven Prayers.* "Abdul and Ebenezer" in *Esquire.*

1977   *Spit in the Ocean,* no. 3, including third part of *Seven Prayers.*

1978   *Spit in the Ocean,* no. 4, including fourth part of *Seven Prayers.*

1979   *Spit in the Ocean,* no. 5, including "Search for the Secret Pyramid" and fifth part of *Seven Prayers.* "The Day After Superman Died" in *Esquire.*

1980   *The Day After Superman Died.*

1981   *Spit in the Ocean,* no. 6, including sixth part of *Seven Prayers.* Trip to China to cover Beijing Marathon.

1982   "Running Into the Great Wall" in *Running.*

Chapter One
From Oregon to California
A Family of West-Walkers

Ken Kesey's *One Flew Over the Cuckoo's Nest* (1962) was a critical success from the beginning. Its popularity, particularly among young people, grew steadily, and its sales surpassed a million by the beginning of the 1970s, when it became the contemporary novel most frequently used in college courses. Because it serves so well as a text, American Fulbright professors have used it in teaching abroad and furthered its recognition. It was adapted as a Broadway play and later as an award-winning film starring Jack Nicholson, adding to its fame. Kesey's second novel, *Sometimes a Great Notion* (1964), has not been nearly so popular, mainly because its complex style demands more of the reader. It, too, was made into a film with well-known actors—Paul Newman and Henry Fonda—but the adaptation was only moderately successful, artistically and commercially. Aside from his novels, Kesey attained notoriety as a style-setter for much of the West Coast psychedelic set in the 1960s. As a leader of the Merry Pranksters, described by one newspaperman as a "day-glo guerilla squad for the LSD revolution in California," he turned from writing to search for new forms of expression induced by psychedelic drugs. He and the Pranksters traveled across the country and back in a bus painted with bizarre designs and startling colors, and thus spawned a host of outrageous vehicles, mobile hippie units, that took to American highways in the late 1960s. Tom Wolfe's *The Electric Kool-Aid Acid Test* (1968) chronicles Kesey's search for new awareness and the escapades of the Merry Pranksters, conferring upon him an almost legendary stature as the charismatic leader who transformed the Beats into the hippies.

In April 1965 he was arrested in California for possession of marijuana and became embroiled in legal actions for the remainder of the year. In January 1966 he was arrested again. Fearing stiff prosecution as a second offender, he fled to Mexico but returned after about six months and was arrested in San Francisco. Eventually he served sentences totaling about five months in the San Mateo County Jail and later at the San Mateo County Sheriff's Honor Camp. Upon release he moved to a farm in Pleasant Hills, Oregon, near Eugene, where he has remained.

Kesey's Garage Sale (1973), with an introduction by Arthur Miller, is a miscellaneous collection of essays, drawings, letters, interviews, and prose fiction by and about Kesey. The longest section is *Over the Border,* a movie script based on his flight to Mexico. Periodically, he has published a magazine called *Spit in the Ocean,* containing installments of a novel in progress titled *Seven Prayers by Grandma Whittier.* These items and the two stories in *Esquire* constitute the main part of his literary output since *Sometimes a Great Notion.*

Ken Kesey's career as writer and cultural hero can best be understood in relation to two geographical locations: western Oregon and the San Francisco Bay area. These are the centers for the important shaping influences in his life; and just as he traveled back and forth between these places, his interests and values have fluctuated. In his life and in his fiction a tension between these two poles is evident. In a way, it is a tension between country and city, but it also is a tension between family roots and individual discovery; between traditional Christian values and those of a new counterculture; between respectability and outlawry; between old ways and rural life and day-glo paint and amplified rock music; and between the straight and the drug cultures. Kesey's life was transformed when he went to Stanford. It was a radical transformation, but he never lost the ties with home and family and the values connected with them.

Ken Elton Kesey was born on 17 September 1935 in La Junta, Colorado, the son of Fred A. and Geneva (Smith) Kesey. One more son was born three years later, Joe, who goes by Chuck. Ken's father had a small creamery business. When the war began he enlisted in the navy and was told he would be called into service soon. The call did not come immediately, and Fred Kesey was not a man suited to restless waiting. He took his family to Eugene, Oregon, to visit with his parents until he was inducted into service. They left Colorado in November 1941, and he was not called into the navy until August of the next year. During that time he went to work in a creamery in Eugene, a job he returned to after the war. During his first year in the navy, while he was at sea, his wife and two sons returned to Colorado to live. Then the family was united at Mare Island near San Francisco, where Fred Kesey was stationed as a refrigeration expert. In 1946 they returned permanently to the Eugene area to continue in the dairy business.

Ken's family, both the paternal and maternal lines, were farmers and ranchers. Like the Stampers described at the beginning of *Great Notion,* they gradually migrated west, "a stringy-muscled brood of restless and stubborn west-walkers." They were not pioneers or visionaries doing the Lord's work or blazing trail for a growing nation; they were simply a restless clan looking for new opportunities. What was essentially the pattern of Kesey's own ancestors, he uses and gives symbolic perspective in *Great Notion.* In the case of Kesey's family, the movement was from Tennessee and Arkansas to Texas and New Mexico, then to Colorado, and finally to Oregon.

Kesey once described his father as "a kind of big, rebellious cowboy who never did fit in. . . ."[1] What he meant by not fitting in is uncertain, because Fred Kesey was a well-liked leader in the dairy business, an officer in dairy organizations, an appealing yarn-spinner, and beloved by his family. Perhaps he meant that his father was a self-sufficient individual and an independent thinker. He was a sort of hero to Kesey, a man he identified with the John Wayne image. Both Kesey and his father were strong-minded, and this, as is the usual case, produced some friction; but he retained great admiration for his father until the latter's death in 1969.

Fred Kesey loved the outdoors. He was the kind of man who considered it "something extra" when he caught a fish. He had his sons on the rivers and in the woods with him from their early years, and they took to it with enthusiasm. Ken's experiences while trout and salmon fishing and duck and deer hunting were an important part of his young years, and he naturally drew upon them when he began writing fiction to serve strategic functions in both *Cuckoo's Nest* and *Great Notion.*

The family also liked physical competition: wrestling, boxing, racing, whatever needed proving. Sundays were often spent at Grandfather Kesey's farm, where Ken arm-wrestled and played with his brother and cousins. He has said that his father believed a time comes when a son should whip his father. It is an important and delicate matter. "A boy has to *know* he can best his father, and his father has to present him the opportunity. It's got to be the right way and at the right time—when the boy really *needs* to make his pitch. He's got to know he can outrun, outwrestle, outlove, *outanything* his old man. My father's a wise man and he gave me the chance. Perhaps this is a father's most significant duty."[2] Kesey's unpublished novel "Zoo" contains a description of such a fight, in which a young man returns to Oregon from living in North Beach in San Francisco and slugs it out with his poultry-farmer father. And, generally in his fiction, father-son relationships are significant. This is particularly true of *Cuckoo's Nest* and *Great Notion*.

At those Sunday gatherings at Grandpa Kesey's, Kesey probably did a good deal of listening also. Plenty of anecdotes and yarns were exchanged, told in a colorful rural vernacular rich in homely but arresting similes and analogies. This talk, an outgrowth of a long tradition of frontier American oral storytelling, shaped Kesey's patterns of expression. His fiction is markedly vernacular and filled with oral anecdotes and tales. The stories told by MacMurphy and old Henry Stamper, for example, resemble those that make up the rich heritage of western American tale-swapping. Kesey himself has a habit of expressing himself in little anecdotes or parables of a downhome flavor. When he has a concept to express, it usually comes out in narrative wrapping. For example, when asked once if he were writing for posterity, he said *no* and then qualified his answer by describing a stream that ran through his yard when he was a boy. Someone had covered it over with mortar and stone so that it looked like the trail of "a seven hundred pound mole." When the stream dried up, he and his brother explored the tunnel and found an old accordion in it. Since it no longer was playable, they took it apart. In a corner among the valves and bellows, they found a note that said, "What the hell you looking in here for, Daisy Mae?" "Well," he says, "I achieved some kind of *sartori* [sic] right there— knowing that *somebody* had *sometime* a very *long* while ago *gone* in there and put that *sign* in that accordian [sic], and he's betting all the time that *someday* somebody's going to come along and *find* it. A mystery for people to wonder about. Well, that's what I want for my books."[3]

One family source of vernacular stories was Kesey's grandmother Smith, a spunky, self-reliant woman who is still living at eighty-nine.

She was the model for Grandma Whittier, the narrator of his novel currently in progress, sections of which have been appearing periodically in *Spit in the Ocean*. In the first section, Grandma Whittier tells in ungrammatical but colorful vernacular a fictionalized version of Grandmother Smith's experience when she was injured in a fall as a child. While the doctor attended her, her spirit sailed out of her body to heaven. There she was met by a tall angel with an enormous book, who, after checking her name, said, "You have been marked by the Blood of the Lamb of God Almighty and you aren't due up here for another good seventy-seven years! The Son of Man Hisself has you down for not less than one entire century of earthly service."[4]

Kesey has said he is "a hard shell Baptist, born and raised."[5] His grandmother Smith accounts for a good deal of that Baptist influence; and although Kesey's parents were not regular churchgoers, their values and standards were Baptist. Grandmother Smith was a churchgoer and an avid reader of the Bible. Whether due to her example or not, Kesey has had a great fondness for the Bible and has frequently recommended it to others. In his enumeration of tools (books, people, and things of special significance to him) in *The Last Supplement to the Whole Earth Catalog* (reprinted in *Kesey's Garage Sale*), the Bible heads the list.

Family stories may have fueled his imagination and his fascination with the fanciful, which manifested itself early in his life. He was drawn to products of the imagination or fancy, the exciting and mysterious things just out of reach of ordinary experience. In an unpublished essay he discusses the *just* and *only* in such expressions. He tells of walking as a boy with his dog across the endless rolling prairies near La Junta, Colorado. When he heard a far-off rumbling coming out of the clouds, he thought it was a herd of wild horses one grandpa or the other had told him about—"with teeth like rows of barbwire and eyes like polished steel balls an' breath that'd peel paint." When he told his mother about it, she said, "It's just thunder, honeybun. You was only imagining you saw the horses." As a man he now asks, "But why, Mama, is it *just thunder?*" And he wonders as he drives across Colorado "What would still roam these prairies if the old creatures had been allowed to breed and prosper, if they hadn't been decimated by that crippler of the imagination: *only.*" He suggests that fact and fiction blend well and both are essential in presenting "the True Happening of the moment." Merely to report as a camera does is just touching the surface. It is like panning the stream instead of digging for the vein. "The vein lies under the topsoil of external reality; it is not hidden. We've known of it for ages, this vein, but it has been put down so long by *just,* disparaged so long by *only,* that we have neglected its development." In reality, this vein is our greatest resource—"this deposit of Grandpa bullshit that we try to turn into a reclamation project as we mature."

He goes on to suggest that mining that vein has many advantages. In writing, for example, "it can mean that as much emphasis can be placed on hyperbole, metaphor, simile, or *fantasy* as on actual events." Or just in "plain old vanilla living" it can mean new strength and discovery. He concludes that "in the vast seas between red and white blood corpuscles Captain Nemo still secretly pilots his Nautilus, this white-haired scourge of Oppression and Warfare. Why not give him his head? Or through the dense growth of neurons, Lou Wetzel stalks the Zane Grey Indians, silent as moss until he strikes with a chilling war whoop. Why not let him stalk?"[6] Such attitudes are undoubtedly behind the claim by Bromden, the narrator in *Cuckoo's Nest,* that what he tells is "the truth even if it didn't happen."[7]

This defense of the imagination is a manifestation of a search or quest Kesey has engaged in. The quest is unique only in the particular experiences through which it has led him. The essential impulse is common and perennial, an instinct present to one degree or another in almost everyone. In Kesey the impulse is particularly strong. He once mentioned this search in an interview. As a boy he had sent for some decals of Batman comic-book characters. The package arrived containing a bonus, a small book of magic. He became interested in magic and later ordered a catalog of stage illusions: "I got into a lot of theatrical magic and did shows all through high school and in college. I went from this into ventriloquism (and even had a show on TV), and from ventriloquism into hypnotism. And from hypnotism into dope. But it's always been the same trip, the same kind of search."[8] In this search lies the explanation for how a straight-living small-town boy of Baptist background, voted most likely to succeed in high school, successful athlete, Woodrow Wilson scholar, became a style-setting leader of a psychedelic counterculture movement.

Prompted by his imaginative penchant for fantasy, mystery, and spiritual adventure, Kesey did lots of reading as a boy. His father read a good deal, mostly popular literature, and specifically Zane Grey. Kesey may have been influenced by his father's reading habits because he says he did not read many important things until high school and college. He enjoyed the books of Zane Grey and named his son after him. Edgar Rice Burroughs is another author he mentions specifically. He says he also went through plenty of comic books and some science fiction. Eventually he discovered serious literature and developed a respect for the classics. He is glad that he had to memorize passages from the Prologue to *The Canterbury Tales* in his high-school literature class and advocates Shakespeare and Milton for students even if they find them difficult. "Let's face it," he told a writers' conference, "for most people, if you don't learn Shakespeare in high school, you'll probably never really get a hit at it."[9] He has been interested in and often critical of the reading lists in his local high schools. He has even made the statement to college audiences that students should not be studying his novels; they should be studying books like the Bible and *Moby-Dick.*

Kesey attended high school in Springfield, a city adjacent to Eugene. There he played guard on the football team, wrestled, and involved himself in other school activities. He was good at decorating and making sets for plays and assemblies, and others enjoyed working with him because of his jokes and humorous commentary. He was in demand to write skits and routines for programs. He did a little writing for the school paper, but chafed under space restrictions. Although he wrote a little poetry, his principal interest was not writing; his first love was acting. In addition to his magic, ventriloquism, and hypnotism, he performed as an actor and won the best-thespian award.

It was while he was working on decorations for a seventh-grade activity that he first met Faye Haxby, who had just transferred from Idaho. They were sweethearts in high school and married on 20 May 1956, the spring before their last year in college. Faye had gone to Oregon State and commuted there to finish her schooling after they were married.

His interest in acting was strong enough that he majored in Speech and Communications when he enrolled at the University of Oregon. After his senior year in high school and his freshman year in college, he spent the summers in Hollywood seeking parts in films. Although he never landed such a job (he thought the agent lost interest when she learned he would be returning to school at the end of the summer) he performed in plays and worked on movie and television sets. He wrote home about seeing "The George Gobel Show" filmed and he watched some of the making of *The Ten Commandments*. In August 1955, with youthful enthusiasm, he wrote his parents, "I'm learning a lot down here—not just movie stuff, but stuff about people." No doubt that environment had plenty of "stuff" to teach a young man from rural Oregon. He became acquainted with some personalities unlike any he had encountered before.

Campus Wonder-Boy

Kesey attended college at the University of Oregon near his home, graduating in 1957. He later described his activities in college as "playing campus wonder-boy." He played football only during his freshman year and then focused his attention on wrestling, eventually receiving the Fred Lowe Scholarship as the outstanding college wrestler in the Northwest. During his senior year, he went undefeated in conference matches, but dislocated his shoulder in the AAU tournament and placed second.

His interest in wrestling has persisted. After college he continued to train at the San Francisco Olympic Club and participated in the Olympic eliminations in 1960, just failing to make the Olympic team. His sons have wrestled in high school, and he has done volunteer coaching. The floor of the main room of the converted barn he and his family occupy is covered with a wrestling mat rather than a carpet. He recently won a medal for his weight class in the forty-two to fifty age group in a state tournament for wrestling coaches.

Kesey's wrestling, the culmination of physical competition he had engaged in since childhood, has had an influence upon his writing. The main characters in his novels are physically strong and imbued with a keen sense of competition. They are self-reliant men out to prove something, unwilling to concede defeat even against overwhelming opposition. Perhaps they are a blending of the western hero and the highly competitive athlete. The two strains are clearly apparent in Hank Stamper, the main character in *Great Notion*.

Kesey pursued his interest in acting in college, and drama and theater were an important part of his Speech and Communications major. He participated in plays and won another thespian award. He liked putting on costumes and becoming someone else. On one of the tapes in the Kesey Collection, he describes doing tryout routines, dressing up using a random assortment of costumes and ad-libbing in a freewheeling way. He said he liked best to do strong, fast-talking, extroverted characters. His description of the type makes one think immediately of Randle McMurphy, and his love of costumes and performance and his training and practice in impersonation partly explain the remarkable costumes and antics of Kesey and the Merry Pranksters described by Tom Wolfe in *The Electric Kool-Aid Acid Test.*

In addition to acting, his major led him to radio and television writing. The Kesey Collection includes several scripts for dramas and documentaries done for a course taught by Dean Starlin. Part of the assignments was to state explicitly the theme. Later, whether the result of this training or not, Kesey made a habit of writing out his themes at the early stages of composing. He seems also to have developed an interest in the methods of film and film writing that influenced his later writing. His novels, particularly *Great Notion,* display devices similar to cinematic techniques—fade-ins, flashbacks, simultaneous action in different locations, etc. The main item in *Kesey's Garage Sale* is a screenplay titled *Over the Border.*

His habit of beginning with theme and his acting experience are both reflected in a statement he made in answer to an interviewer's question about how he created characters: "I studied acting and I was taught to interpret a character by figuring out, from a detailed exam-ination of his behavior, exactly what he *wanted.* The theory there is that everything a man does springs from his motivations. In writing, I find myself reversing the process: I know, to *start* with, what a character wants: he exists for me as a kind of abstract creature who wants a specific thing. So, by figuring out how he *gets* what he wants, I learn about the sort of man he is."[10]

His friends in Drama could not understand why he was on the wrestling team and associated with athletes; and of course his friends among the athletes could not understand why he would involve himself with the theater group. But in fraternity activity he was able to blend his interests and talents. As a member of Beta Theta Pi, he participated in numerous activities ranging from intramural sports to songfests and talent shows. In the late 1950s most extracurricular activities of the

University of Oregon revolved around the fraternities and sororities. Kesey was in the thick of them. His talents made his fraternity a consistent winner in song, skit, and decorating competition. He also had talent for fraternity pranks. One of his first attempts at the short story during college, "The Great Slingshot Campaign," describes water-balloon battles between fraternities, inner tubes serving as catapults.

It was not until college that Kesey attempted to write fiction. Some stimulation to do so must have come from his course work, particularly the class in radio and television writing. But most of his stories were not written specifically for classes. The manuscripts that have been preserved are annotated by teachers, but often this occurred because he would take what he had written to someone in the English Department and ask for a critique. James Hall—now a distinguished writer and critic at the University of California at Santa Cruz—was particularly helpful and encouraging.

Since many of the short-story manuscripts in the Kesey Collection are undated, it is difficult to determine which were written at the University of Oregon and which were written later while he was at Stanford. The manuscripts display the usual clumsiness and experimentation characteristic of the beginning writer, but they also reveal imaginative power. One of the best, "Cattail Bog," has the flavor of Faulkner and Flannery O'Connor. It is narrated by the wife of a child molester. The man takes a little girl into the cattails and brings her back dead. The dialect, the simple-minded narrator, and the horror suggest the influence of what has been called Southern Gothic. "The Gentle Jock" is the story of a physically powerful but sensitive and emotionally vulnerable athlete. In "The Calliope" a big country boy is tempted to leave home to wrestle in a carnival but stays to care for his widowed mother. "The First Sunday of September" is set in a lumber town on the Oregon Coast; a visiting young man is drowned in a swim race with a tough old woman locally renowned for her swimming prowess. In "The Avocados" two University of Oregon students visiting Los Angeles pick up Mexican girls and take them out to eat. At the restaurant are two Indian men whom the students eventually leave the girls to help. The point of the story is the contrast between the girls, who, like avocados, are soft on the outside but hard inside and the Indians, who are associated with the apple of the prickly pear: hard and prickly outside but soft and sweet inside. "The Mountain Year" tells of a father and son who come into town, start a fight that eventually involves everybody in the vicinity, and then get into their truck and go home. There are also some science-fiction stories written for a writing class.

This apprentice work is not exceptional, but it reveals some of the themes and settings that later appear in Kesey's published work and demonstrates that he was beginning to take a serious interest in writing and becoming curious about the techniques of fiction and the power of language. By the time he graduated in 1957, he had decided to become a writer. While working for a year at the family creamery, he wrote his first novel, "End of Autumn," about college athletics.

With all of his campus activities, Kesey managed to maintain excellent grades due to his remarkable intelligence. According to his mother, he had scored in the genius category on his IQ tests taken in elementary school. He had impressed his teachers enough that he was recommended for a Woodrow Wilson Fellowship. He was not in a position to work toward the M.A. in English because he had not majored in English and lacked the necessary background courses; so when he did receive the Wilson Fellowship, he chose to enroll in the creative-writing program at Stanford.

Perry Lane

The notice of the Woodrow Wilson Fellowship arrived in the same mail with a letter from the Selective Service classifying him 4F due to the shoulder injury sustained in the AAU wrestling tournament. He had been worrying about having to go into the army and had toyed with the idea of going to Coast Guard school. Now his plans were clear, and he entered the creative-writing program at Stanford in the fall of 1958.

He studied under Wallace Stegner and Richard Scowcroft and with visiting instructors Malcolm Cowley and Frank O'Connor. Apparently, Stegner emphasized the importance of point of view, because Kesey mentioned that emphasis several times in his correspondence. For example, in a letter to Ken Babbs he wrote that "Wally [Stegner] may have been much more correct than us avanting guards wanted to give him credit for—maybe the largest problem in fiction *is* PV." Both of Kesey's novels are remarkable from the standpoint of point of view. On one occasion he submitted to Stegner a paper titled "On Why I Am Not Writing My Last Term Paper." It was the kind of thing every English teacher receives from time to time from students feeling restricted by the usual assignments. They justify their failure to do the assignment on the basis that it was not challenging or meaningful enough. Stegner would have none of it. He chided Kesey in his annotation and said the paper was self-expression, which is really self-indulgence. "Now go write that novel, but don't for God's sake let it turn into self-expression."

Cowley taught the writing seminar in the fall of 1960. Kesey was in the class unofficially, a courtesy extended to former fellows. He was working on what would become *Cuckoo's Nest*. Cowley describes him as having "the build of a plunging halfback, with big shoulders and a neck like the stump of a Douglas fir." He was excited by discovering something original in Kesey's manuscript and they discussed it in private sessions. Cowley claims not to have contributed a single sentence. "Probably I pointed out passages that didn't 'work,' that failed to produce a desired effect on the reader. Certainly I asked questions, and some of these may have helped clarify Kesey's notions of how to go about solving his narrative problems, but the solutions were always his own."[11] When asked in an interview in 1963 what he had learned from Cowley, Kesey replied, "Well, before Cowley, I studied with James Hall at Oregon. He taught me how *good* writing can be. Cowley taught me how good a writer *I* could be."[12]

According to Cowley, Kesey did not like the way O'Connor (in private life Michael O'Donovan) conducted the class the next semester and stopping coming. Kesey invited other members of the class to meet at his house for conversation. This was in the winter of 1961. By this time, says Cowley, "He had become the man whom other young rebels tried to imitate, almost like Hemingway in Montparnasse during the 1920s."[13]

More important to Kesey's development than any particular teacher was the interaction with other students. He was in seminars with a number of talented young writers, including Larry McMurtry, Robert Stone, Wendell Berry, and Peter S. Beagle. The students would take turns reading from their work and receiving suggestions and criticism from other members of the seminar. Among intense young writers, this situation can often lead to tensions and conflict, but in this case a spirit of helpfulness usually prevailed. Kesey feels he learned a great deal from these discussion sessions.

In the first of these seminars, he met Ken Babbs. The first time he saw him he thought, "If this gorilla can make it through the class, then surely I can." They were soon close friends and have continued to be so; Babbs was a kind of lieutenant to him during the Merry Prankster years and now has a farm near Kesey's. When Babbs joined the marines, the two corresponded regularly. By mutual agreement the letters were practice in writing and to be preserved for each other. In them they experimented with style and tone, offered suggestions and criticism, described their writing projects, and talked about writing theory. They also sent each other manuscripts for evaluation and comment. The letters display a mutual respect for each other's writing talent and are encouraging and supportive. In a way they extended the kind of interchange the two had experienced in their Stanford seminars.

However important Stanford course work was for Kesey, its impact cannot compare with the transformation in his life wrought by his experiences at Perry Lane. This was a one-block-long area of small cottages in unincorporated Menlo Park, near the Stanford golf couse. The Lane had a Bohemian tradition of long standing; Cowley refers to it a Stanford's Left Bank. In the late 1950s and early 1960s it became a center for Bohemian life patterned after Beat living in San Francisco's North Beach, just forty miles away. Writing of Perry Lane in 1968, Vic Lovell, the friend to whom *Cuckoo's Nest* is dedicated, described what was going on there: "We pioneered what have since become the hall-marks of hippy culture: LSD and other psychedelics too numerous to mention, body painting, light shows and mixed media presentations, total aestheticism, be-ins, exotic costumes, strobe lights, sexual mayhem, freakouts and the deification of psychoticism, eastern mysticism, and the rebirth of hair."[14] The pioneering claim in this list of questionable distinctions may be overblown, but the statement probably indicates fairly accurately the kind of cultural radicalism taking shape there. The Lane was like a club and not easy to get into. Those living there were involved with each other intimately. Lovell says, "In very serious jest we used to get stoned and recite, deads pan: 'I pledge allegiance to Perry Lane, and to the vision for which it stands.'"[15]

It was Robin White, author of *Elephant Hill*, who introduced Kesey to Perry Lane and helped him get a cottage there. On a tape describing this period, Kesey refers to him as "the person who changed my life." On another tape (recorded probably in the early 1960s), he says Perry Lane was the most important world for him: "all that came before led up to it; all that comes after will be the result of it."

At Perry Lane they considered him a diamond in the rough. He has described himself at that period as "a jock, never even been drunk but that one night in my frat house before my wedding and even then not too drunk—just a token toot for my brothers' benefit. . . ."[16] His wife and mother corroborate this, except that they were unaware of the fraternity-house incident. In the Lane he was introduced to wine drinking, marijuana smoking, wife swapping, and a variety of new attitudes and practices. This was the time of the San Francisco Renaissance and the Beats. Kesey visited North Beach and read such things as Jack Kerouac's *On the Road*, William Burroughs's *Naked Lunch* (published excerpts as early as 1959), and Clellan Holmes's *The Horn* (which he described in a letter to a friend as "the best jazz book I've ever read, and truly made me feel a thing for jazz I've always known other people to feel but was sure I was missing"). It was an exciting period of discovery for him. He wanted to be a writer and these radical attitudes and this unconventional behavior seemed the perfect subject matter. The remarkable thing is how rapidly and thoroughly he absorbed the entire scene. He was soon wearing a beard; playing the guitar and singing folksongs; baking marijuana cakes (principal ingredient grown secretly on the golf course in Menlo Park) and making tapes to listen to while eating them; thinking of opening a coffee house serving nutmeg tea rather than coffee, the tea reputed to have an effect similar to marijuana; and writing a novel about North Beach. It was not long before he was considered a trend setter rather than a diamond in the rough.

The most significant discovery for him came when, at Vic Lovell's suggestion, he volunteered for drug experiments being conducted at the Veterans' Hospital in Menlo Park. He was paid to take a number of hallucinatory drugs, one of which was LSD, and report in detail their effects. Later, he took a job as aide at the hospital. The hospital work provided inspiration and material for *Cuckoo's Nest,* and the drug experiments set him on a course of personal experiments with drugs, searching for ways to heighten consciousness. That search resulted in the famous acid tests described by Tom Wolfe.

The novel about North Beach is titled "Zoo," and a section of it won for him the $2,000 Saxton Prize from Stanford. It is reminiscent of Kerouac in many ways, with its wine drinking, drug addicts, jazz musicians, stupid and brutal police, interracial marriages, poverty-level Bohemian living, cars scarred by frantic miles on the highways, and talk of nihilism and Zen. It differs from Kerouac in not being simply autobiographical reporting. Kesey was working deliberately to develop several important themes. Elements of autobiography are present but significantly modified. The main character is a young man from a poultry ranch in Oregon, son of a former rodeo cowboy. As he becomes involved in the life of North Beach, the tension between him and his family increases to a climax. He has to struggle with the choice between a selfish, irresponsible individualism and a recognition of his obligations and responsibilities toward others. The matter is muddled by the rootless and unstable way of life in North Beach.

Kesey submitted the novel without success to several publishers. A section of it has appeared in *Kesey,* a collection of unpublished material and work in progress edited by Michael Strelow and the staff of *Northwest Review.* [17] Page 233 of the manuscript, near where the excerpted section begins, has the following note handwritten around the top, bottom, and margins:

Chapter called "Don't wrestle with a tarbaby . . ." just now picked out of old North Beach novel called *"Zoo"* that I claimed was never published because, at that time, five or so years ago: "the name 'beatnik' has too much meaning now in the pacific eye—too much to overcome, I think . . ." I have been heard to say ". . . I'll wait a number of years for the beat bit to die down before I bring it out." Bullshit. I didn't publish it 5 years ago because nobody bought it. I didn't publish it after success brought requests for it because I kept telling myself I would someday re-write it, bring it up to my *present standards* (like who wants their old adolescent bumbles marring the grace of present *mature* standards and fucking up a hard-won reputation?) . . . more bullshit. I am a terrible liar. But at least this present inky lie is straight-shootin' enough to bygod warn ya about it. [18]

The novel has considerable merit. Its weakness perhaps results from Kesey's youthful fascination with a life-style so radically new to him. But it should be noted that *On the Road* is filled with the same adolescent fascination with unconventional behavior. In its artistic modification of autobiography in the interests of theme, "Zoo" is probably superior to *On the Road*.

Whatever its intrinsic merits, "Zoo" has value for understanding Kesey's development. It embodies the Oregon-California polarity that has determined his career as writer and public figure—the tension between downhome conventional values (family, farming, Christianity) and a counterculture of experiments in expanding consciousness through drugs and uninhibited self-expression and indulgence. And it manifests the transforming impact of his experience on Perry Lane.

Kesey planned to write a novel about Perry Lane. In the Kesey Collection under the title "One Lane" are eighty pages of story outline and talking with himself about what he is trying to do. He planned to combine two themes: (1) "Everybody has a dragon in their house," and (2) "The Prometheus Myth." In a stream-of-consciousness method of sketching out the novel (a method he used in the first stages of his published novels) he notes what he wants to accomplish and how it can be done. Here is a sample: "This is the time when I can best state the existing problems, because I am not doing a scene, but am being an all-knowing God. I can travel around like a ghost, like a baron-god-ghost, like Thomas in 'Under Milk Wood' and see the people, their doings and goings, their thoughts and dreams. Time is lumped into a chapter. I am not telling a scene, I am telling a compilation of scenes and situations and status quos. I am montaging the Lane, timelessly." Occasionally he identifies a technique or effect as the kind Steinbeck or Faulkner uses. Most frequently he alludes to those of Nelson Algren, a writer of special interest to him at this time. His preoccupation with point of view and his conscious formation of literary strategy are apparent throughout.

The Keseys lived at Perry Lane until 1963, when a developer bought most of it, served notice to the residents, and bulldozed the cottages. The residents were greatly upset and angry, for they felt a way of life, a radical culture, was being destroyed along with the buildings. Vic

Lovell, for example, made this comment about "the fall of Perry Lane": "It ended with creativity turned to distraction, ecstasy turned to psychosis, and commitment turned to nihilism."[19] This rather melodramatic comment is probably the result of feelings generated among a community of impressionable young people who had experienced together a lively period of cultural change. Kesey was particularly distressed by the destruction of the Lane. He had experienced a remarkable era of creativity while living there, and momentous changes had occurred in his interests and values. As a writer he has known no comparable period of productivity and may never do so again. Along with short stories and the eighty-page plan for "One Lane," he had written three novels, one of them large and unusually complex.

With money earned by *Cuckoo's Nest* he bought a place at La Honda and moved there to begin a remarkable new phase in his career.

Chapter Two
One Flew Over the Cuckoo's Nest

Breadth of Appeal

One Flew Over the Cuckoo's Nest has had a broad appeal. Its language and situations offend some, particularly among parents and schoolboards. Others are offended by its treatment of women and blacks. Some find it simplistic in philosophy; and some find its plot, setting, and characters too carefully contrived. But it continues to appeal to a wide audience, including literarily sophisticated readers. It is one of few works to achieve acclaim in three forms: novel, play, and film. The play, written by Dale Wasserman, appeared on Broadway starring Kirk Douglas in 1963 and was revived in 1971. Althouth it was unsuccessful there, it has enjoyed continued success on college campuses. The film version in 1975, directed by Milos Forman and starring Jack Nicholson, was a box-office hit and won six Academy Awards.

This success as play and movie as well as novel suggests that the story's themes are fascinating and congenial to a contemporary audience. When the novel appeared in 1962, it supplied a critique of an American society that was portrayed in the serious media of the 1950s as consisting of a lonely crowd of organization men, offered affluence only if willing to pay the price of strict conformity. That critique continued to suit the mood of the 1960s and 1970s because larger themes were involved: the modern world as technologized and consequently divorced from nature; contemporary society as repressive; authority as mechanical and destructive; contemporary man as victim of rational but loveless forces beyond his control; and contemporary man as weak, frightened, and sexless. The novel's apparent message that people need to get back in touch with their world, to open doors of perception, to enjoy spontaneous sensuous experience and resist the manipulative forces of a technological society was particularly appealing to the young, but not just to them. An admiration for self-reliant action runs deep in the American psyche. Ruth Sullivan, in a psychological analysis of the novel's appeal, suggests that it gives the reader an opportunity to feel the self-pity of being unjustly persecuted. Americans feel oppressed by Big Goverment and the novel provides them justification. And the self-pity is enhanced by the antiestablishment tone. The novel "richly gratifies latent or conscious hostile impulses against authority," and also satisfies the tendency to depend upon strong, heroic figures and "to feel unjustly treated (masochistic and moral-righteousness pleasures)."[1]

Besides embodying engaging themes, the novel for most readers is a pleasure to read. It is filled with comic language and incidents. Randle Patrick McMurphy is a vivid, unforgettable character; Big Nurse is an eminently hatable villain; and the perennial conflict of Good and Evil is reenacted with sufficient suspense to generate lively interest.

Another reason for the novel's appeal is that it treats or touches upon a wide variety of subjects, issues, and disciplines. *Lex et Scientia,* the official organ of the International Academy of Law and Science, devoted an entire 100-page double issue to essays on *Cuckoo's Nest,* which the editor describes as "a cornucopia of source material from disciplines so numerous and varied as to challenge the mind and imagination."[2] It reaches, he says, into such areas as psychology, psychiatry, medicine, literature, human relations, drama, art, cosmology, and law and even carries overtones of religion, American culture, and folk-culture. And it does this with a mixture of tragedy, pathos, and humor. It is not surprising that the novel has been used as a text for courses in a variety of subjects and disciplines. Sociologists, for example, are interested in it because, as Doctor Spivey within the novel points out, Big Nurse's ward is "a little world Inside that is a made-to-scale prototype of the big world Outside."[3] An essay by sociologists explaining how it can be used in a sociology course lists these topics for discussion: the phenomenon of power; the reality of the social; patterns of integration; personal organization; social organization; patterns of differentiation; social/cultural change; and societal institutions.[4] Psychology, English, and American Studies departments have found it equally rich in thought-provoking topics.

The variety of interests it has attracted is of course paralleled by the variety of responses it has evoked. Here is a partial list of phrases and topics that show up in treatments of *Cuckoo's Nest*: the patterns of romance, the patterns of comedy, the patterns of tragedy, black humor, the absurd, the hero in modern dress, the comic Christ, folk and western heroes, the fool as mentor, the Grail Knight, attitudes toward sex, abdication of masculinity, the politics of laughter, mechanistic and totemistic symbolization, the comic strip, ritualistic father-figure, the psychopathic savior. The list could easily be extended. Although the novel has elements of comic-strip exaggeration and oversimplification, it touches upon root motives and conflicts that have many branches. Readers will continue to focus on the branch or branches attracting their immediate interest.

Inspired by the Tragic Longing of Real Men

Much of the inspiration for *Cuckoo's Nest* came from Kesey's experiences at the Veterans' Hospital in Menlo Park. He went there first as a paid volunteer for government experiments with "psychomimetic" drugs. He was given drugs and asked to record exactly how they affected him. Kesey was well suited in several ways to be a subject for such experiments. He had a natural and lively curiosity about what the human mind is capable of; and he was particularly interested in the visions, inspirations, and creative consciousness that might lie just beyond ordinary thinking and dreaming. For the sake of his own personal research, as it were, he was probably more interested in the experiments than were those conducting them. Along with this willingness, he possessed an unusual ability to register impressions and express them; he had a highly developed imagination and considerable verbal skill. At times, however, his talent for writing down his impressions was wasted because of the effects of the drug. After sitting in a room for an hour or so rapidly recording what he considered to be remarkable impressions and insights, he would later discover that what he had written was gibberish. But when the particular drug or dosage allowed him to be reasonably coherent, he had the verbal power to convey vividly the flux of impressions exploding in his mind. When he later turned from writing novels to concentrate on achieving heightened consciousness and perception through psychedelic drugs, he used a technique similar to that used in these first volunteer experiments. Many of the tapes in the Kesey Collection are of him recording, as they occur, his impressions under drugs. They display singular skill in vivid spontaneous description. Similes, so necessary in conveying an unusual, dreamlike experience to others, come fluently and are often strikingly evocative. It is likely that the fantasies or hallucinations described by Chief Bromden, the narrator of the novel, are modeled after ones Kesey had experienced in the hospital experiments.

After the experiments concluded, Kesey continued at the hospital as a psychiatric aide. He has said that McMurphy was "inspired by the tragic longing of the real men I worked with on the ward."[5] His midnight-to-eight shift allowed him periods of five or six hours, five days a week, during which he had nothing to do but a little mopping, buffing, and checking the wards with flashlight. He used this time for writing his novel. The taped conversations with friends in which he describes his work at the hospital reval how much of his own experience went into the novel, transformed to one degree or another. He had unpleasant encounters with rigid and demanding nurses; he scuffled once with a black aide; he attended patients with a variety of peculiar behavior patterns; and he observed generally how a psychiatric ward functions. A letter to Babbs, written when Kesey was completing four weeks of training as an aide, describes several patients he worked with. The exact characteristics and phrases of some of these patients appear in the novel.[6] According to Wolfe, he arranged for someone to give him, clandestinely, a sample of shock therapy so he could describe it firsthand.[7]

Kesey says some of the novel was written while he was under the influence of drugs. The most notable instance is the first few pages, in which he created the narrator. "I was flying on peyote, really strung out there, when this Indian came to me. I knew nothing about Indians, had no Indians on my mind, had nothing that an Indian could even grab onto, yet this Indian came to me. It was the peyote, then, couldn't be anything else. The Indian came straight out from the drug."[8] This example is of special importance because his decision to have Bromden tell the story was perhaps the most significant one he made in writing the novel. Most critics agree that his treatment of point of view is a masterstroke.

There is something disingenuous, however, about Kesey's claim of drug-generated inspiration. Maybe the phrase concerning knowing about Indians requires qualification; there are many degrees of knowing. As a matter of fact, Kesey did know a good deal about Indians and had thought and written about them. For an assignment in his radio and television writing class at Oregon he had written "Sunset at Celilo," a script about an Indian who returns from the Korean Conflict at a time when the dam was being built at The Dalles and his tribe was being forced to leave their village. An interviewer reports Kesey's telling of "an Indian in a logger's camp suddenly crazed with the recollection of his blood and racing headlong from the mountain side to attack with his knife the grillwork of a diesel hurtling down the highway paved through his grandfather's land, dying out there bravely and badly, living again in the idea for Chief Broom Bromden, the narrator of *One Flew Over the Cuckoo's Nest*. . . ."[9] On tape he tells about playing football on the same team with a large Indian, about an Indian who had worked for them, and about an Indian he had once seen with lipstick all over his face, his cowboy shirt spattered with blood. And mention has already been made of the unpublished story "The Avocados," which sympathetically treats two displaced Indians. It may be that Kesey was looking so anxiously for evidence that drugs could expand consciousness, partly as a justification of his drug experimenting and proselytizing, that he attributed too much to the peyote.

Wherever the inspiration for Bromden came from, it was a fortunate one and Kesey did remarkable things with it. The point of view in the novel is an unusual achievement. On the one hand, Bromden fantasizes. This gives the reader a singularly vivid impression of the emotional and psychological state of the patients. The novel is about rescue or salvation, and Bromden's inner condition gives us a clear idea of what the patients need rescue from; and the exaggeration in his fantasies also spotlights and emphasizes the matters important to theme. For example, the phantom machines Bromden describes in the walls and in people are part of a significant pattern of imagery used to develop the central theme concerning technological manipulation. But at the same time Bromden is an unreliable witness he is also an extremely reliable one. We feel he tells us the truth about McMurphy;

in fact, he tells it with such penetration and insight that it has a consistent and coherent shape and meaning for us. The combination of hallucination and truth in the narration is a notable stylistic accomplishment. Fact and fantasy alternate, but the reader has no difficulty distinguishing one from the other, and thus they successfully complement each other.

Kesey began working on the novel using a more conventional first-person narrator. In a letter to Babbs, he mentions, "I tried working on the novel you have now [*Cuckoo's Nest*] from the PV of an aide, me, and realized how much the narrative sounded like other promisingyoungwriter narrative." He did not want this. He was aiming at a narrator—he lists Holden Caulfield, Benjy Compson, Gulley Jimson (of Joyce Carey's *The Horse's Mouth*) and Humbert Humbert as examples —who leaves the ground and lives and breathes in print.

In a letter to Kirk Douglas, he explains that Bromden's point of view is necessary

to make the characters *big enough* to be equal to their job. McMurphy, as viewed from the low-angle point of view of the Chief, is a giant, a god, he's every movie show cowboy that ever walked down a mainstreet toward the OK corral, he's every patriot that ever died for his countrymen on a scaffold in history books. The Big Nurse is seen more clearly by the Indian than by anyone else, as that age-old ogre of tyranny and fear simply dressed in nice neat white. Of course, McMurphy and the nurse are also people, in a human situation, but in the distorted world inside the Indian's mind these people are exalted into a kind of immortality. To do this you need fantasy. You need to jar the reader from his comfortable seat inside convention. You need to take the reader's mind places where it has never been before to convince him that this crazy Indian's world is *his* as well.

Thus the distortion or exaggeration in the novel is deliberate, and is created by manipulation of point of view.

Kesey's choice of Bromden as narrator allows for a hero of event and a hero of consciousness; McMurphy is the former and Bromden the latter. When these two are juxtaposed, each is better delineated. John W. Hunt has pointed out that "Kesey's use of the single narrator who is telling a story deeply important to his own understanding of himself forces the reader to follow a double story line, one centering upon the tale told and the other upon the teller and the telling." In this regard the novel resembles other American novels that raise the question "whose story is this?"—*Moby-Dick, The Great Gatsby, Absalom, Absalom!*[10] As Bromden tells McMurphy's story, he comes to understand himself better and eventually regains control of himself and acquires sufficient strength to flee the institution and face the world once again. Hunt explains that an examination of the two stories reveals an exchange of visions, "a clash between the originally tragic view of Bromden, to which hope has been added, and the hopeful view of McMurphy, which became completely qualified by tragedy from the day he signed on for the whole game."[11] By using Bromden, Kesey not only has a vehicle for telling McMurphy's story, he has a center of consciousness for interpreting and judging it and a specific example of the significance of it.

An unpublished story written after Kesey began work at the hospital reveals a transitional stage between "Zoo" and *Cuckoo's Nest.* The main character of "The Kicking Party" is a jazz musician, a North Beach type with goatee and a drug habit. He is a mental patient who one of his fellow patients says is "plotting to undermine the whole system with his evil laugh and sinful stories." The head nurse watches him "through her protective glass shield from her sterilized isolation booth." He tells "heightened, hilarious stories of jazz days or junk days or juice days." The undermining of the system, the laughter and stories, and the head nurse suggest *Cuckoo's Nest*; but at this point Kesey is still caught up with Beat life. The Beat response to an uncongenial conformist society was withdrawal by such means as wine, pot, jazz, and Zen. Kesey's temperament was not suited for withdrawal. He grew up admiring strength and responding to competition. It was natural that his background and inclinations would eventually bring his creative energies to focus on an active and self-reliant character like McMurphy rather than on a jazz musician like the one described in "The Kicking Party." Moreover, the point of view in the story is conventional; he had yet to discover a narrative key like Bromden. In the story the laugher and the mental patient are a single person. The turning point would come when he separated them as hero of event and hero of consciousness.

"He Sounds Big"

Cuckoo's Nest is dedicated to Vic Lovell, "who told me dragons did not exist, then led me to their lairs." In explaining to Gordon Lish what he meant by this, Kesey said that Lovell had "argued against the existence of spiritual dragons," or in other words, against a spiritual realm of experience, one transcending ordinary life and rational explanation. But, ironically, it was Lovell who arranged for him to participate in the drug experiments, which he believed introduced him to a new realm of experience.[12] The dedication is a reflection of his persistent fascination with the transcendent, his impatience with the attitude that dreams are *only* dreams and imaginative experiences are *just* fictions. His introduction to drugs was a major phase in the search that began in childhood with his interest in magic.

Cuckoo's Nest appears more experimental and unconventional than it actually is. The tone is irreverent and antiestablishment, and the psychotic Indian narrator is original; but for the most part Kesey has made skillful use of well-established techniques and patterns. He draws upon the most familiar of myth patterns—the savior and sacrificial hero, death and rebirth, and the search for the father. He also alludes frequently to popular types from American folk tradition and popular culture. His patterns of imagery are unmistakably explicit and developed in conventional ways, and the structure of the novel is clear and symmetrical. The novel's success results from a skillful application of established literary methods to an apparently iconoclastic theme. The iconoclasm is more apparent than real because the Establishment is largely caricatured and the values asserted are basically those at the heart of Western American culture.

The opposition of Nature and Machine is the primary conflict of the novel, and this opposition constitutes the central nervous system for the patterns of imagery. The narrator, Bromden, who is really only half Indian, represents the man of nature. As a patient in a mental institution, he is a victim of the Combine, the forces of technology and human manipulation whose avatar is Miss Ratched, the Big Nurse. Just when Bromden, overcome by feelings of fear and futility, is at the point of succumbing to the Combine, the boisterous McMurphy arrives as a kind of profane savior preaching the gospel of laughter, the first principle of which is self-reliant strength. The central conflict is a singular version of the archetypal struggle between the forces of good and evil or freedom and bondage in which victory is achieved through the intervention of a savior or sacrificial hero.

The novel is divided into four parts of cycles of action that are approximately parallel in structure. At the beginning of each cycle the Big Nurse is either ascendant or biding her time incubating a new strategy of attack, and at the end McMurphy or what he represents is ascendant. There is a progression in the movement from cycle to cycle, however, for despite setbacks, McMurphy by the end of each part has brought Bromden closer to the freedom from fear that constitutes his salvation. The climax comes in Part 3, and Part 4 is falling action or denouement.

The first section of Part 1 introduces most of the major themes and images. The Combine is mentioned and Big Nurse and her minions are introduced through images of technology and machinery. The Big Nurse's name, Ratched, suggests "rachet" (a mechanism consisting of a notched wheel, the teeth of which engage with a pawl, permitting motion of the wheel in one direction only). This name alone goes a long way in suggesting her impersonal singleness of purpose. From the viewpoint of the narrator, who drifts in and out of hallucinatory states, she has "equipment" and "machinery" inside; "she walks stiff"; her gestures are "precise" and "automatic"; each finger is like "the tip of a soldering iron"; she carries a wicker bag filled with "wheels and gears, cogs polished to a hard glitter" (4); when she is angry she blows up "big as a tractor"; her face is "smooth, calculated, and precision-made, like an expensive baby doll, skin like flesh-colored enamel." The only apparent mistake in her manufacture is her "big, womanly breasts" (5). But these breasts, which would ordinarily represent natural warmth and maternal tenderness, she is bitter about and keeps tightly bound up within her stiff starched uniform. Her black orderlies also have "equipment" inside and their eyes glitter out of their black faces "like the hard glitter of radio tubes out of the back of an old radio." Bromden interprets their mumblings as the "hum of black machinery, humming hate and death" (3).

After these images of mechanization and manipulation are introduced in the first section, they are used consistently in describing Miss

Ratched and everything in her charge. She is a dedicated "adjuster" who wants her ward to run "like a smooth, accurate, precision-made machine." She sits in the center of a "web of wires like a watchful robot," tending her network with "mechanical insect skill," dreaming of a world of "precision efficiency and tidiness like a pocket watch with a glass back" (26–27). The ward is a factory for the Combine, very similar in Bromden's mind to a cotton mill he had once visited. This factory fixes up mistakes made in the neighborhoods, schools, and churches, and Miss Ratched is pleased when a "completed product" goes back into society as "a functioning, adjusted component." The chronic patients are "the culls of the Combine's product"—"machines that can't be repaired" (14). Sitting before her steel control panel, the Big Nurse controls and manipulates the patients, who are described variously as "arcade puppets" (30), "mechanical puppets" (35), and "shooting-gallery targets" (48). Because of years of training, the three black aides are no longer controlled by direct wires; they are on the Big Nurse's frequency and manipulated by remote control. If a patient is troublesome, he can be fixed by receiving a new "head installation." An obstreperous patient named Ruckly received this kind of overhaul and returned with eyes "all smoked up and gray and deserted inside like blown fuses"; after that he was "just another robot for the Combine" (15–16).

These images are the product of the narrator's fear-distorted imagination. They are abundant in the first section because at this point his fear is intense. Kesey wants to establish clearly in the beginning what victimization by the Combine means— fear, paranoia, weakness, and disorientation from nature. Bromden mentions a fog machine. When he loses touch with reality and his hold upon his individual personality and spiritual strength weakens, the fog increases. Throughout the novel the fog serves as a barometer of his emotional and psychological state and thickens and dissipates according to the fluctuations of his mental and spiritual health.

Just as the first section establishes the pattern of imagery consistently associated with the forces of the Machine or Combine, it also introduces a set of images or motifs linked with nature. In an attempt to control his fear, Bromden tries to remember things about his village on the Columbia River and about hunting with his father. These recollections are the first of a number of references to or reminiscences of life in the outdoors that identify him as a man of nature. His inordinate fear of machines, revealed so emphatically in his fantasies, accentuates his being a man whose natural element is the outdoors, where life is simple and unrestrained. The supporting motifs for this characterization are the dog and the sense of smell. In the first section, the dog is "out there in the fog, running scared." He sniffs in every direction but "picks up no scent but his own fear, fear burning down into him like steam" (7). The parallels between Bromden and the dog are obvious. He has a keen sense of smell, which at first produces only fear as he smells the machinery inside the Big Nurse, but which later begins to register natural odors as he recovers.

According to Ronald Billingsley, the images function in six major ways: "they make of the narrative a concrete presentation; they serve as a device of foreshadowing; they give the language the feel and effect of poetry; they give a reflexive power to the flashback sequences; they serve to more accurately define character; finally, they help to objectify theme."[13]

When the contrasting imagery of Machine and Nature is identified, the battle lines for the central conflict are readily apparent. The determining force in that struggle is Randle Patrick McMurphy, who is introduced in the second section. His initials (R.P.M.—revolutions per minute) suggest the motion and energy characteristic of his personality. He is thirty-five, has never been married, and is a wanderer up and down the West. He has worked as a logger and as a carnival wheel man. Mostly he has been in and out of jail for brawling, disturbing the peace, and repeated gambling. He has been committed by the state from the Pendleton Correction Farm. He looks upon the change as relief from hoeing peas and an opportunity for finding new suckers to fleece. When he is introduced, and repeatedly throughout the novel, he is likened to an auctioneer or carnival pitchman. He is brassy, vulgar, and fast-talking. A significant item in his description is that he received the "Distinguished Service Cross in Korea, for leading an escape from a Communist prison camp" (42). But, characteristically, he afterward received a dishonorable discharge for insubordination. He will prove insubordinate in the mental ward and in essence lead an escape. On two occasions he will liken the Big Nurse's ward to a Chinese Communist prison and her methods to those used there (64, 268). In a letter to Babbs, written while Kesey was at work at the hospital, he mentions he has just been called upstairs to listen to a tape about the brainwashing of Korean War prisoners. "It was most enlightening, especially in terms of the book I'm writing. It had a lot to do with the 'Code of Conduct.' Remember it? we used to ridicule it upstairs in the ROTC office at Stanford? Well, I'm becoming very square or something—but I'm beginning to believe the code has a lot to it, a lot about strength. Strength is the key. We need strong men." In both of his novels, the main theme is this need for strong men.

Bromden realizes immediately that the new man is no ordinary Admission. He does not "slide scared down the wall" or submit meekly to the aides. "He sounds like he's way above them, talking down, like he's sailing fifty yards overhead, hollering at those below on the ground. He sounds big" (10). Throughout the story Bromden uses size as a metaphor for emotional strength. Later, he refers to McMurphy as "a giant come down out of the sky to save us from the Combine . . ." (255). And when through McMurphy's "special body-buildin' course" Bromden has grown, one of McMurphy's female friends describes him as "A Goliath—fee, fi, fo, fum" (285).

The characteristic of McMurphy that is emphasized when he is introduced and that takes on increasing significance as the story unfolds is his laughter. His laughter "is free and loud and it comes out of his wide grinning mouth and spreads in rings bigger and bigger till it's lapping against the walls of the ward" (11). Bromden suddenly realizes it is the first real laugh he has heard in years. Everyone in the ward, patients and staff, is stunned by it; and "even when he isn't laughing, the laughing sound hovers around him, the way the sound hovers around a big bell just quit ringing—it's in his eyes, in the way he smiles and swaggers, in the way he talks" (11).

McMurphy's hands are also given prominent and frequent mention. He makes a point of shaking everybody's hand when he arrives. This human touching contrasts with the cold and sterile treatment the patients receive from Big Nurse, but there is more to it than this. Along with his laughter, his hand symbolizes his strength and represents his power to save. It becomes a helping hand indeed. Bromden says at a climactic point near the end of Part 1, "It is like . . . that big red hand of McMurphy's is reaching into the fog and dropping down and dragging the men up by their hands, dragging them blinking into the open" (134). When McMurphy leads the patients out of the hospital on a fishing trip and they are intimidated by a service station attendant, "He put his hands up in the guy's face, real close, turning them over slowly, palm and knuckle. 'You ever see a man get his poor old meat-hooks so pitiful chewed up from just throwing the *bull*? Did you, Hank?'" (225). Those hands represent action and assertion, just the qualities the patients lack. The effeminate hands of Harding are played off against those of McMurphy. Until he benefits from McMurphy's example, Harding is embarrassed about his hands (described as doves) and keeps them hidden in his lap. After he has found strength and the courage to take the initiative, he uses his hands forcefully and unself-consciously to shape and emphasize what he says (293).

Another thing that should be noted about McMurphy's introduction into the novel is that Bromden links him with his father—"He talks a little the way Papa used to . . ." (11). His father was chief of the tribe and at one time an object of his son's admiration. He was "big" in his eyes. But the Combine made him small and weak. Part of the reason Bromden is in the hospital is the debilitating disillusionment he experienced observing what happened to his father: "But when I saw my Papa start getting scared of things, I got scared too . . ." (160). The frequent connection between McMurphy and his father suggests Bromden's need for a strong father figure, someone who can demonstrate that fighting against the Combine is not futile. This will restore him to the way of life he knew while his father was strong, a life close to nature.

At the beginning of Part 1, Big Nurse is in full control. Bromden is mute (feigning deafness) and completely intimidated. The degree to which fear and a feeling of futility have loosened his grip on his manhood and sanity is revealed in his paranoid fantasies of the fog and the terrifying, ubiquitous machinery. His sense of smell, which links him to the world of nature, registers only the odor of oil and heated machinery. And the other patients are in no better condition. When McMurphy arrives with "that big wide-open laugh of his," he is immediately a disruptive force: "Dials twitch in the control panel" and the Acutes "look spooked and uneasy when he laughs" (17). There is no place for laughter in the Big Nurse's smooth-running machinery of manipulation, and the patients have been conditioned to the point where they are afraid of laughter. Harding, as a spokesman for the inmates, explains to McMurphy just what that brawling Irishman will be up against if he decides to fight Miss Ratched and her machinery. In the middle of his presentation, Harding attempts an ironic laugh, but "a sound comes out of his mouth like a nail being crowbarred out of a plank of green pine" (60). His forced and grotesque "squeaking" is the nearest thing to real laughter that the patients are capable of producing. McMurphy, in an attempt to generate some resistance against Miss Ratched, calls attention to the patients' fear, telling them they "are even scared to open up and *laugh*. You know that's the first thing that got me about this place, that there wasn't anybody laughing. I haven't heard a real laugh since I came through that door, do you know that? Man, when you lose your laugh you lose your *footing*. A man go around lettin' a woman whup him down till he can't laugh any more, and he loses one of the biggest edges he's got on his side" (68). Harding answers that he does not think laughter is an effective weapon against "the juggernaut of modern matriarchy" and challenges McMurphy to try his weapon of laughter against Miss Ratched. McMurphy accepts the challenge, after it has been made more attractive by the wager of five dollars from each of the other patients, and begins his calculated campaign to "bug" Miss Ratched "till she comes apart at those neat little seams, and shows, just one time, she ain't so unbeatable as you think" (72).

McMurphy's campaign against Miss Ratched in Part 1 awakens some hope within Bromden, and he begins to establish control of himself again. This change is marked by a renewed ability to smell natural odors, a reawakened recognition of the power of laughter, and finally an escape from the fog machine.

Just after McMurphy has momentarily staggered Miss Ratched by an impudent display of his flashy underwear (black satin shorts with big white whales on them—a gift from a female literature major who said he was a symbol), Bromden sweeps under McMurphy's bed and gets a smell of something that makes him realize for the first time since he has been in the hospital that although the dorm had been filled with many odors, not until McMurphy came was there "the man smell of dust and dirt from the open fields, and sweat, and work" (98). Soon after this, again while sweeping, Bromden notices a picture of a fisherman on a mountain stream that he thinks must have been brought in when the "fog" had been too thick for him to see it. He imagines himself walking right into the picture and says, "I can smell the snow in the wind where it blows down off the peaks. I can see mole burrows humping along under the grass and buffalo weeds" (122). This reawakened sensitivity to the world of nature, his home environment, is a positive sign that Bromden is developing a resistance to the machine world of the hospital.

After watching McMurphy humorously needling one of the black aides, Bromden feels good and remembers how his father once did much the same thing with some government men who were negotiating to buy off a treaty. His Papa had made them look ridiculous in the eyes of the Indians who had all "busted up laughing fit to kill." "It sure did get their goat; they turned without saying a word and walked off toward the highway, red-necked, us laughing behind them. I forget sometimes what laughter can do" (92). Bromden observes McMurphy closely and apprehends his strategy. McMurphy takes everything calmly and observes the humor in the behavior of the hospital personnel—"and when he sees how funny it is he goes to laughing, and this aggravates them to no end. He's safe as long as he can laugh, he thinks, and it works pretty fair" (113).

The climax of the first part comes with the vote concerning television time. When he raises his hand in that vote, Bromden takes the first action that commits him to fight back against the Combine. Even as he raises his hand he thinks, "I wouldn't do it on my own." He thinks McMurphy put "some kind of hex on it with his hand" when they shook hands the first day (136). McMurphy's healing influence and touch cause him to act despite his fear. The drama of this incident is intensified by the motif of the fog machine. The fog is a way for Bromden to find safety and comfort from the terrifying reality of life under the manipulative control of the Combine. "Nobody complains about all the fog," he says. "I know why, now: as bad as it is, you can slip back in it and feel safe. That's what McMurphy can't understand, us wanting to be safe. He keeps trying to drag us out of the fog, out in the open where we'd be easy to get at" (123). The tension mounts before

Bromden raises his hand because he goes into one of his deepest fogs: "I feel I'm going to float off someplace for good this time" (128). This is a crisis fog because McMurphy's influence has brought him to face clearly once again the hurt that led him to his disturbed condition. In a flush of sympathy, he understands the pain in the life of one of his fellow patients: "I can see all that, and be hurt by it, the way I was hurt by seeing things in the Army, in the war. The way I was hurt by seeing what happened to Papa and the tribe. I thought I'd got over seeing those things and fretting over them. There's no sense in it. There's nothing to be done" (130). But Bromden cannot resist McMurphy's "big red Hand," which pulls him out of the fog. After the vote, he remarks, "there's no more fog any place" (141). Therefore, by the end of Part 1, although he still has a long way to go, Bromden, through McMurphy's help, has taken the first step toward recovering his autonomy and self-respect. This is made clear by the laughter motif, which appears again on the last page of Part 1. Miss Ratched has lost her composure and Bromden, instead of being afraid, thinks it is funny: "I think how his voice sounds like it hit a nail, and this strikes me so funny I almost laugh" (138). He *almost* laughs; this is all he is capable of at this point. His salvation will not be complete until he can laugh naturally and uninhibitedly.

McMurphy's first major victory, the television vote, results from his unsuccessful attempt to lift a control panel. Bromden notes, "yesterday, before he tried lifting that panel, there wasn't but four or five men might of voted" (134). Why did his attempt make such a difference? The answer lies in the example it provided. "His whole body shakes with the strain as he tries to lift something he *knows* he can't lift, something *everybody* knows he can't lift" (120–21). To the patients— "rabbits" Harding calls them—this manifestation of all-out exertion in an attempt that obviously appears futile is inspiring. It causes them to reexamine their commitment to passive weakness and generates a flicker of hope that asserting themselves might not be futile. And of course the control panel has a symbolic dimension, for although it is not presently in operation, it is a *control* machine and representative of the Combine. Later, McMurphy tells Bromden he will make him strong again so he can lift the panel. He does and Bromden lifts it, and eventually he throws it through the window to obtain his escape. This is an ironic touch since a control panel is used to destroy control, the moral being that dehumanizing technological control is impossible when man remains strong and refuses to submit. The first control panel incident also foreshadows that McMurphy will be able to provide the example but unable to save himself.

There is other careful foreshadowing in Part 1. The case of Ruckly is presented early to suggest what could happen to McMurphy. Because he was "being a holy nuisance all over the place," Ruckly was taken away for treatment and brought back two weeks later, his eyes "all smoked up and gray and deserted inside like blown fuses" (15). McMurphy eventually pays a similar price for making himself a nuisance and is brought back to the ward, his eyes "like smudged fuses in a fuse box" (309). And the case of a Mr. Taber is referred to several times as a foreshadowing parallel to McMurphy. On the whole, Part 1 effectively introduces and sets in motion all the significant elements of plot, theme, and imagery.

"Keep An Eye Out for Old Number One"

At the beginning of Part 2, the results of McMurphy's initial victory are manifest: "all the machinery in the wall is quiet" (141). But the narrator is beginning to comprehend "the full force of the dangers we let ourselves in for when we let McMurphy lure us out of the fog" (142). Miss Ratched returns, "clear-headed," and begins to reassert her control. Her manipulative powers are confidently displayed in the staff meeting at which she persuades the doctor and other staff members that McMurphy should not be sent to the Disturbed ward. She will not agree that he is "some kind of extraordinary being" and wants him left in her ward so she can prove to the other patients he is not. She is afraid the "redheaded hero" will be viewed as a martyr if he is taken away to Disturbed at this point.

But while Miss Ratched is initiating her new strategy to deal with the redheaded hero, it is made clear to us what effect McMurphy's first triumph has had upon the narrator. "For the first time in years," he says, "I was seeing people with none of that black outline they used to have, and one night I was even able to see out the windows." Before he opens his eyes at that window, he smells the breeze. "It's fall," he thinks, "I can smell that sour-molasses smell of silage, clanging in the air like a bell—smell somebody's been burning oak leaves, left them to smolder overnight because they're too green" (154–55). When he opens his eyes he sees for the first time that the hospital is out in the country. Observing the moonlit pastureland reminds him of a night when he was off on a hunt with his father and uncles. All of this is the man of nature coming back to his true self, a reawakening that is emphasized once again by the dog motif. Looking out the window, he sees a gangly mongrel dog sniffing around at squirrel holes, "the breeze full of smells so wild makes a young dog drunk." This dog, who is thoroughly enjoying his freedom and the myriad smells in the night air, contrasts significantly with the bluetick hound of the first section of Part 1, out in the fog, running scared, smelling only the scent of his own fear. The narrator and the dog hear and watch a flight of wild geese overhead. Then the dog lopes off, "steady and solemn like he had an appointment." The narrator holds his breath as he hears a car approaching and watches "the dog and the car making for the same spot of pavement" (156). Before he can see what happens, however, a nurse and orderly put him back into bed. The symbolic significance of this incident is readily apparent: the dog (Nature) and the car (Machine) are on a collision course, but it is too soon at this point in the novel for us to see the outcome. On the last page of the novel, however, we will see Bromden escaping from the grounds of the hospital "in the same direction [he] remembered seeing the dog go."

One of Miss Ratched's most effective tools of intimidation is the threat of indefinite confinement that faces a patient who has been committed. After a conversation with the lifeguard at the pool, McMurphy realizes for the first time the full implications of that threat and becomes fully conscious of his vulnerability. Immediately thereafter he puts aside his rebelliousness and becomes pliable and cooperative. Bromden is quick to observe this change and is afraid: "The white tubes in the ceilings begin to pump their refrigerated light again . . . I can feel it, beams all the way into my stomach" (164). With McMurphy ending his resistance, Miss Ratched is in charge once again. "Whatever it was went haywire in the mechanism," remarks Bromden, "they've just about got it fixed again. The clean, calculated arcade movement is coming back . . . in the Nurses' Station I can see the white hands of the

Big Nurse float over the controls" (170). The clearest sign that McMurphy is retreating is the loss of his ability to laugh; this is the very danger he had warned the others against earlier. It is appropriate that this reversal is linked with the control panel where he had previously displayed his determined strength. Now, playing cards near the control panel, he loses his self-control when Martini kids him, "and the cards splash everywhere like the deck exploded between his two trembling hands" (176). These hands are of course what the other patients depend on.

He is bewildered as he begins to realize that it is something more than the Big Nurse that is responsible for the trouble there. "I don't seem able to get it straight in my mind," he says (180). He does gradually get it straight in his mind, however, and comes to understand that it is not just the Big Nurse but also the Combine that he must fight. He eventually understands also that although he has been committed, many of the other patients have not; therefore, while his struggle can only destroy himself, it may save others. He ultimately decides to fight.

But before he decides to fight he undergoes a period of temptation, beginning with his talk with the lifeguard at the swimming pool. Some see a parallel between his test and that of Christ in the wilderness following his baptism. This may be far-fetched but suggests itself because of the more explicit Christ images in the novel. Harding describes the table in the Shock Shop as "shaped, ironically, like a cross" and the patient receives "a crown of electric sparks in place of thorns" (67). Fredrickson accused Miss Ratched of wanting to "crucify" his friend Sefelt, who is described as being pinned to the wall, his hands "nailed out to each side with the palms up" (169). As the group leaves for fishing, Ellis tells Billy to be "a fisher of men" (222). When taken for the shock treatment, McMurphy says, "Anointest my head with conductant. Do I get a crown of thorns?" (270). On McMurphy's way there a patient looks at him and says, "I wash my hands of the whole deal" (266); and another says, "It's my cross, thank you Lord" (269). After Bromden suffocates McMurphy, Scanlon asks, "Is it finished?" (309). McMurphy's healing hands, his leading twelve people to the sea to fish, his sacrifice of himself—these and other things according to one's interpretive ingenuity can be considered Christ images. But one can be well aware of such parallels without taking them too seriously. It is a mistake to do so. Kesey uses them playfully, intending more to excite archetypal reverberations for the action of the story than to make McMurphy restrictively a Christ figure.

His talk with the lifeguard makes him aware of what being committed means. His reaction is to think only of himself. In leaving the pool, he refuses to help a man with hydrocephalus out of the footbath, where he is blowing bubbles in the milky-looking water. Later the same day, he fails to support Cheswick when the latter challenges one of the Big Nurse's policies. The other patients sense immediately that he is no longer standing up for them. Bromden thinks he is finally "getting cagey" like the rest of them: "The way Papa finally did when he came to realize that he couldn't beat that group from town who wanted the government to put in the dam because of the money and the work it would bring, and because it would get rid of the village. . . ." The advantage of being cagey is that "It's safe. Like hiding" (165). But when Cheswick drowns himself after McMurphy's failure to back him up, McMurphy begins to realize that his actions have generated obligations. He has pulled the men out of the fog and increased their vulnerability. A sense of responsibility begins to dawn in his essentially self-centered nature. When Scanlon says, "Hell of a life. Damned if you do and damned if you don't" (170), McMurphy knows what he means. If he continues his campaign against Miss Ratched, the others benefit but he sacrifices his freedom and possibly destroys himself. If he "keeps an eye out for old Number One" (182), he benefits but his fellow patients are lost.

The dog motif appears again at the end of Part 2, this time in connection with McMurphy. As he returns from the building where shock treatments are given, having just heard the treatment described, and consequently knowing the full consequences of continued resistance, Bromden says of him, "I could see that there was some thought he was worrying over in his mind like a dog worries at a hole he don't know what's down, one voice saying, Dog, that hole is none of your affair—it's too big and too black and there's a spoor all over the place says bears or something else just as bad. And some other voice coming like a sharp whisper out of way back in his breed, not a smart voice, nothing cagey about it, saying, *Sic* 'im, dog, *sic* 'im!" (186). The two voices here make explicit the temptation McMurphy is undergoing. In Part 1 his behavior was self-centered showing off. In Part 2 he is brought to realize the obligation the strong incur toward the weak, and he becomes soberly aware of the risk he runs by resistance to what he now understands is more than simply control by a single Big Nurse.

The drama of his reversal, which comes in the last section of Part 2, makes use of a device similar to the fog machine at the end of Part 1. Whereas at the end of Part 1 it was fog that built up in intensity and then disappeared, at the end of Part 2 it is the ringing sound in the narrator's head that builds up to a high pitch and then stops immediately after McMurphy defiantly smashes the window of the Nurses' Station. This action signals that McMurphy has weighed the situation carefully and has chosen to save his fellow patients regardless of the peril to himself.

"McMurphy Led the Twelve of Us to the Ocean"

After passing through his temptation in Part 2, McMurphy begins his saving mission in earnest in Part 3. "The nurse was biding her time till another idea came to her that would put her on top again" (193). Meanwhile, McMurphy organizes a fishing trip that becomes the climax of the novel. Laughter and outdoor nature are the dominant elements in that climactic section.

The first convert to laughter in this part is the narrator himself. McMurphy discovers that Bromden has been chewing gum stuck to the bottom of the bed frames in the dorm. When he begins singing the old song, "Oh, does the Spearmint lose its flavor on the bedpost overnight?" Bromden's first impulse is to become angry, thinking that McMurphy is making fun of him. "But the more I thought about it," he says, "the funnier it seemed to me. I tried to stop it but I could feel I was about to laugh—not at McMurphy's singing, but at my own self. . . . I couldn't help but start to chuckle" (205). At the end of Part 1 he had *almost* laughed; now he does laugh, although it is a rather pitiful performance; "I didn't sound like much because my throat was rusty and my tongue creaked. He told me I sounded a little out of practice and laughed at that. I tried to laugh with him, but it was a squawking sound, like a pullet trying to crow. It sounded more like crying than laughing" (206). This laughter (particularly once he is able to laugh at himself) is the key indicator of Bromden's recovery and is concomitant with the first words he utters since entering the hospital. In fact, it is not until he has laughed that he is able to speak.

In this part we learn why Bromden has been feigning deafness. He recalls that "it wasn't me that started acting deaf; it was people that first started acting like I was too dumb to hear or see or say anything at all" (197). He had first noticed this when he was a boy and three people came to the village to talk to his father, their purpose being to persuade the Indians to leave so the dam could be built. The leader of this trio was "an old white-haired woman in an outfit so stiff and heavy it must be armor plate" (199). This description and other of her characteristics link her with Big Nurse; in fact, Bromden says she spoke in "a way that reminds me of the Big Nurse" (202). And like Miss Ratched she knows how to get her way through cold manipulation, in this instance by using Bromden's mother for leverage in obtaining his father's cooperation. Bromden is amazed that he can remember this incident: "It was the first time in what seemed to me centuries that I'd been able to remember much about my childhood. It fascinated me to discover I could still do it" (203). This reawakening to his past is a sign of health, of course; the only way he will recover mental and emotional stability is by facing such recollections. A contrasting parallel situation from McMurphy's childhood is provided a few pages later. As the only child in a group of bean pickers, he was ignored and therefore gave up talking for four weeks. But finally he opened up and, in characteristic fashion, told them all off, lost the job, but felt it was worth it (206–7).

One of the few references to machinery in this part is the description of what happens when the prostitute whom McMurphy has invited on the fishing trip enters the hospital. "I think apparatus burned out all over the ward trying to adjust to her come busting in like she did—took electronic readings on her and calculated they weren't built to handle something like this on the ward, and just burned out, like machines committing suicide" (219). This is a delightful reversal because the machinery used to "adjust" the patients now must adjust itself and in so doing is destroyed. Machinery is shunted into the background in this part of the novel because nature has the principal role.

It is "a fine woodsmoked autumn day" when they set out to go fishing. All of the patients but McMurphy are frightened and ill at ease with their freedom and are therefore pliable victims for the service-station attendants who try to foist unneeded oil filters and windshield wipers on them when they stop to gas up. The doctor is with them. Because he is dominated by Miss Ratched, he needs McMurphy's cure as much as the patients do. McMurphy's bravado saves the situation at the service station and inspires the group with at least the appearance of self-confidence; but without the ability to laugh they have no real strength: "I think McMurphy knew better than we did that our tough looks were all show, because he still wasn't able to get a real laugh out of anybody. Maybe he couldn't understand why we weren't able to laugh yet, but he knew you can't really be strong until you can see a funny side to things" (227). The condition of the narrator and the other patients is objectified in the description of the little boy from one of the "five thousand houses punched out identical by a machine and strung across the hills outside of town" whom they see always at the end of the game of crack-the-whip: "He'd always be so scuffed and bruised that he'd show up out of place wherever he went. He wasn't able to open up and laugh either. It's a hard thing to laugh if you can feel the pressure of those beams coming from every new car that passes, or every new house you pass" (228).

Bromden's tension at passing through a region with so many signs of the Combine at work dissipates when he is aboard the fishing boat and heading out to sea. "When we passed the last point of the jetty and the last black rock, I could feel a great calmness creep over me, a calmness that increased the farther we left land behind us" (233). It is here at sea, away from the hospital, which is "the Combine's most powerful stronghold," that the process of salvation through laughter reaches its climax. McMurphy observes the group's uninhibited outdoor activity—the enthusiasm over fish caught, the tangled lines, the shouting and cursing—and begins to laugh: "Rocking farther and farther backward against the cabin top, spreading his laugh out across the water—laughing at the girl, at the guys, at George, at me sucking my bleeding thumb, at the captain back at the pier and the bicycle rider and the service station guys and the five thousand houses and the Big Nurse and all of it. Because he knows you have to laugh at the thing that hurt you just to keep yourself in balance, just to keep the world from running you plumb crazy" (237–38). McMurphy knows there is a painful side (this is something the narrator has doubted up until this moment), but he has a balanced view about it: "He won't let the pain blot out the humor no more'n he'll let the humor blot out the pain" (238). The laughter becomes infectious and takes on cosmic proportions in this moment of epiphany:

It started slow and pumped itself full, swelling the men bigger and bigger [size, it will be remembered, is the metaphor used repeatedly to signify self-reliant strength and dignity]. I watched, part of them, laughing with them—and somehow not with them. I was off the boat, blown up off the water and skating the wind with those black birds, high above myself, and I could look down and see myself and the rest of the guys, see the boat rocking there in the middle of those diving birds, see McMurphy surrounded by his dozen people [his disciples], and watch them, us, swinging a laughter that rang out on the water in ever-widening circles, farther and farther, until it crashed up on beaches all over the coast, on beaches all over all coasts, in wave after wave after wave. (238)

After this moment of transformation, this Pentecost, the group radiates a new aura of self-assurance that is immediately apparent to the loafers on the dock: "They could sense the change that many of us were only suspecting; these weren't the same bunch of weak-knees from a nuthouse that they'd watched take their insults on the dock this morning" (242).

Bromden, in particular, is greatly strengthened by this experience and restored to a sense of harmony with nature, from which the machines have separated him for so long. "I noticed vaguely that I was getting so's I could see some good in life around me. McMurphy was teaching me. I was feeling better than I'd remembered feeling since I was a kid, when everything was good and the land was still singing kid's poetry to me" (243). But this strength that Bromden and the others have acquired has been tapped from McMurphy; so at the same time Bromden remarks on the positive change within himself, he also remarks on the exhaustion apparent in McMurphy, whose face reveals him as "dreadfully tired and strained and *frantic,* like there wasn't enough time left for something he had to do . . ." (245). This is the sacrificial hero evidencing the cost of his sacrifice and a sense of urgency concerning his mission.

"No More Rabbits"

The day after the fishing trip, Big Nurse has her next maneuver underway: she will try to discredit McMurphy by persuading the patients his motives have been entirely selfish and mercenary. Kesey frequently uses irony in the mouth of Miss Ratched. Early in the novel she calls McMurphy a "manipulator," just as her own powers as a manipulator are being forcefully revealed (25). Now she insists he is not "a martyr or a saint" (252), just as he is indeed proving himself to be a kind of martyr or saint. But for a while her insinuations about his selfish motives have the desired effect. Even Bromden has doubts when McMurphy uses him to win unfairly a bet concerning lifting the control panel. All doubts are allayed, however, when McMurphy takes George's side against Washington, one of the black aides: "right at that time all of us had a good idea about everything that was going to happen, and why it had to happen, and why we'd all been wrong about McMurphy" (259). McMurphy precipitates the fight "sounding more tired than mad," and everybody could hear "the helpless, cornered despair" in his voice (261). This is a premeditated act, done almost reluctantly from a sense of duty. McMurphy has weighed the consequences.

That he acts out of a sense of responsibility is emphasized shortly after this when Bromden and McMurphy are taken to Disturbed as a result of the fight. Bromden is struck by the faces there, which reveal a need and a hunger for help, and he wonders "how McMurphy slept, plagued by a hundred faces like that, or two hundred, or a thousand" (266). During the mental struggling of Part 2, McMurphy had mentioned in answer to Harding's question about what he saw in his dreams that he saw "nothing but faces, I guess—just faces" (175). These and other references to faces are used to clarify McMurphy's motivation. Near the end this motivation is made explicit when Harding says it is the weak (the patients) who drive the strong (McMurphy) into seemingly crazy acts of self-sacrifice (295) and when Bromden says it was the patients' need and not simply defiance of Big Nurse that determined his actions: "It was us that had been making him go on for weeks, keeping him standing long after his feet and legs had given out, weeks of making him wink and grin and laugh and go on with his act long after his humor had been parched dry between two electrodes" (304–5). McMurphy eventually gives us his own distinctive facial expression as a sacrifice for others. When he is brought back to the ward after the lobotomy, Bromden says, "There's nothin' in the face," and Scanlon agrees that it is "too *blank*" (308).

Part 4 resolves the main themes and patterns of imagery. Bromden's salvation is complete enough that he can withstand the test of shock treatment: "It's fogging a little, but I won't slip off and hide in it. No . . . never again. . . . this time I had them beat" (275). When he smashes the control panel through the window to obtain his freedom, "the glass splashed out in the moon, like a bright cold water baptizing the sleeping earth" (310). Bromden's recovery and rebirth are central because he is a special representative figure. He has been there longer than any of the other patients; he was the farthest gone of any capable of recovery; and he is the most closely identified with nature. Member of an ethnic minority, he represents those most subject to victimization; but, significantly, he is the one with the most potential strength. And in addition to Bromden, Harding demonstrates that he too has found himself through McMurphy's example.

There is another spectacular laughing scene when the girls and the liquor are smuggled into the hospital itself. This laughing scene is a modulation of the one on the fishing boat and is necessary as a part of the falling action of the plot, in order to demonstrate that the patients are now able to laugh within the stronghold of the Combine as well as in the open freedom of nature. The laughter signifies the defeat of Miss Ratched: "Every laugh was being forced right down her throat till it looked as if any minute she'd blow up like a bladder" (297). As the laughter swirled around her, the "enamel-and-plastic face was caving in. She shut her eyes and strained to calm her trembling, concentrating. She knew this was it, her back to the wall" (301). McMurphy's last defiant act, ripping open the Big Nurse's uniform and exposing her breasts, "bigger than anybody had ever even imagined, warm and pink in the light" (305), is a final attempt to release the natural from the perverted restrictions of a regimented and mechanistic system. Miss Ratched returns in a new white uniform, but "in spite of its being smaller and tighter and more starched than her old uniforms, it could no longer conceal the fact that she was a woman" (306). Yet McMurphy himself is defeated; his work as savior is consummated by the sacrifice of himself, but his saving mission succeeds. Even after he is gone, his "presence" is "still tromping up and down the halls and laughing out loud in the meetings and singing in the latrines" (307).

"The Juggernaut of Modern Matriarchy"

By skillfully drawing upon proven conventions within the literary tradition—a timeworn yet timeless pattern of myth, a conscious and elaborate manipulation of images, a standard conflict-and-resolution plot with hero and villain—Kesey has created a novel that in terms of the social or cultural tradition is highly unconventional. His degree of formal skill is noteworthy among recent novelists and gives *Cuckoo's Nest* a significant place in recent fiction. Most critics acknowledge this formal excellence, but some are troubled by the novel's treatment of women and blacks. The rising popularity of the book coincided with the rising influence of the women's movement, and this situation has produced the principal controversy regarding the novel. Many of the women in *Cuckoo's Nest* are portrayed as domineering, manipulative, and emasculating. Miss Ratched is the principal offender, but her characteristics are echoed in the woman who leads the group desiring the dam, in Bromden's mother, in Billy's mother, and, to some extent, in Harding's wife. The only woman treated sympathetically aside from the prostitutes is the Japanese nurse. Harding announces the novel's primary view of women when he says, "We are victims of a matriarchy here, my friend, and the doctor is just as helpless against it as we are" (61).

Many feminists have expressed guilt for having actually enjoyed the novel when they first read it prior to "liberation." One woman in a symposium on *Cuckoo's Nest* said, "It's the real dinosaur vision of the relationships between the sexes. It reinforces a large number of negative stereotypes that are very present in our culture anyway. They slide in so noiselessly because we're taking such pleasure in the different, more human liberation with which we identify, that we are not even aware of them, and that's why I use the word 'dangerous' about the novel."[14] Leslie Horst argues that the novel portrays women who violate social expectation as unnatural and evil, while those who are pliable and fit the male view, as do the prostitutes, are portrayed as good. The message is that good women cannot be threatening or powerful. "Not only is the portrayal of women demeaning, but considerable hatred of women is justified in the logic of the novel. The plot demands that the dreadful women who break rules men have made for them become the targets of the reader's wrath."[15] Elizabeth McMahon argues that "The Big Nurse happens also to be the Big Victim when viewed with an awareness of the social and economic exploitation of women."[16] She suggests that Kesey should have been sympathetic and understanding toward Big Nurse's point of view. Ruth Sullivan provides a Freudian interpretation in which Miss Ratched is Big Mama, McMurphy is Big Daddy, and the patients are Little Sons, it is an Oedipal triangle marked by a man-woman power struggle. The sons are taught that mature women are dangerously intent on emasculating men.[17] Raymond Olderman finds that Kesey's "flat portrayal of women and of blacks is more stereotypic and uncomfortable than funny or fitting with his cartoon character pattern. It borders too much on the simplistic."[18] In a particularly caustic attack on the novel, Robert Forrey insists that "The premise of the novel is that women ensnare, emasculate, and, in some cases, crucify men."[19]

Cuckoo's Nest puts into sharp relief some important issues concerning feminism and literature, serving as a special case in this regard. Many feminists concede that the novel is artistically successful but are outraged by the sexism they see in it. This raises questions about whether the problem lies with Kesey or with a narrow feminism. And these questions lead to considerations about the author's freedom: to what extent does programmatic feminism infringe upon artistic freedom?

The antifeminist charges have naturally generated counterarguments. Ronald Wallace argues that such charges are based on two faulty assumptions: "first, that the novel is a romance, and second, that McMurphy is its hero, fully embodying its values." He says *Cuckoo's Nest* is not a romance but a comedy. It does have the typical romantic antitheses: self/society; primitive/civilized; freedom/control; heart/mind. But its final wisdom is that of high comedy and its primary method is reversal of expectation and inversion of values. "To fault Kesey for his treatment of women and blacks is to miss the comedy of a device that has informed comic art from Aristophanes to Erica Jong, the reversal of traditional roles." The reversal of human and mechanical and traditional male-female roles is a comic indication of the world being out of joint.[20]

Another counterargument is based on an interpretation of the novel as tragedy. That it is read as romance, comedy, tragedy, satire, and several other things is a tribute either to its richness as an object of criticism or to the ingenuity of critics. In any case, Michael Boardman argues persuasively that *Cuckoo's Nest* has tragic power and is related to the great tragedies of all ages because it portrays a conflict that is not merely between individuals but is inner. As in Shakespeare's tragedies, the struggle between Big Nurse and McMurphy becomes a fight between two opposed principles in McMurphy's being. McMurphy, like Hamlet, must become something other than what he was before the disaster or tragic victory. According to this argument, the antifeminine element that some readers have found objectionable is "local" rhetoric designed to allow the reader to experience McMurphy's tragedy as moving and significant. "For the dramatic requirements of the story," says Boardman, "Nurse Ratched had to be very nearly an incarnation of evil, unthinking or otherwise. For Mac's struggle to seem important, the forces opposing him must not be too 'understandable,' and never sympathetic. . . . A little understanding, where villains are concerned, often courts disaster; with Big Nurse, as with Iago, the moral terms of the struggle need to be clear in order to prevent confusion."[21] Consequently, to have made Big Nurse more "human," more understandable, as McMahon suggested Kesey should have done, would have been to attenuate the force of the tragic action.

Ronald Billingsley acknowledges that women serve as antagonists for the men in the novel but insists that the real conflict is not one between men and women. "It would be a serious mistake," he says, "to read the novel as the work of a misogynist. Big Nurse and her emasculating ilk are no more truly feminine than the Acutes and Dr. Spivey are truly masculine. Like machines, these women are neuter, asexual devices that respond to *power.*"[22] Statements from the novel such as the following support this interpretation: Big Nurse walked past McMurphy, "ignoring him just like she chose to ignore the way nature had tagged her with those outsized badges of femininity, just like she was above him, and sex, and everything else that's weak and of the flesh" (150–51). Miss Ratched is a villain not because she is a woman, but because she is not human. McMurphy's ripping open of her shell-like uniform is not a revengeful attack on a castrating bitch: it is a symbolic gesture indicating that the human must be liberated from the machine if the oppression of the Combine is to be eliminated.

Kesey himself feels that the charges of sexism in *Cuckoo's Nest* are unwarranted. He insists his motives, conscious or unconscious, were not those attributed to him by feminist critics. Some biographical information is pertinent to the controversy. One of the Kesey tapes records a conversation at a party in which Kesey is telling about his experiences working at the hospital. Another man who did similar work is present. They both agree that the white nurses were usually hard, tough, and trying to prove something. The black nurses were different. The nurse in "The Kicking Party" and Big Nurse are undoubtedly shaped largely out of Kesey's experiences with nurses as an aide. The kind Japanese nurse in *Cuckoo's Nest* perhaps had her origin in the black nurses he knew. Consequently, Big Nurse may reflect to some extent a "pre-Liberation" female personality of the late 1950s—the woman feeling much alone in asserting herself in a male world and therefore finding it necessary to be overly aggressive and domineering in order to prove her worth.

Responses and Evaluation

Cuckoo's Nest is notable for the variety of interpretive responses it has evoked. As was mentioned above, it has been treated as comedy, most extensively by Ronald Wallace, who believes it is structured on the fertility ritual described by F. M. Cornford in *The Origin of Attic Comedy*. The basic conflict is between two archetypal characters, the *alazon* and the *eiron,* the boastful, self-deceived fool and the witty self-deprecator who pretends ignorance in order to defeat his opponent. In addition to acting as *eiron,* McMurphy functions as "A Dionysian Lord of Misrule" who "presides over a comic fertility ritual and restores instinctual life to the patients."[23] Raymond Olderman interprets the novel as a romance centering on the waste-land theme, in which McMurphy is "a successful Grail Knight, who frees the Fisher King and the human spirit for a single symbolic and transcendent moment of affirmation."[24] Michael

Boardman's interpretation of the novel as tragedy was mentioned in the preceding section. Sheldon Sacks also categorizes it as a "narrative tragedy," pointing out that McMurphy makes choices leading to the lobotomy. "The protagonist's monstrous doom is consequently seen as a victory, and his human quality, though in all conventional ways mundane, unlovely, self-seeking, as one we must newly conceive of as great."[25]

A number of critics have been interested in *Cuckoo's Nest* as a western novel reflecting characters, language, and values associated with the American frontier. Richard Blessing says, "Essentially, the McMurphy who enters the ward is a frontier hero, an anachronistic paragon of rugged individualism, relentless energy, capitalistic shrewdness, virile coarseness and productive strength. He is Huck Finn with muscles, Natty Bumppo with pubic hair. He is the descendant of the pioneer who continually fled civilization and its feminizing and gentling influence." According to Blessing, McMurphy mirrors the classic and popular patterns of American manhood. As a logger, associated with cowboys, he reminds us of Paul Bunyan, Pecos Bill, the Lone Ranger, and the Marlboro man. He is also linked with other American heroic types: the gambler, hustler, confidence man, and the phallic hero of traveling-salesman and locker-room stories.[26] Ronald Billingsley fits the novel into the tradition of southwest humor, noting the element of exaggeration, the tall-tale character, the regional dialect, the bawdy language and racy stories, the emphasis on physical strength, and the oral style. And he explains that "the tall tale comic tradition can be utilized not only for humor, but also for rich character portrayals, social criticism and the explication of significant themes."[27] These vernacular western and folk elements are significant in *Cuckoo's Nest* and are even more apparent in *Great Notion*. They originate in Kesey's family background, his life in Oregon, and his temperament and personality. He admires frontier values, and Gerald Graff is correct in suggesting that underlying the ostensibly iconoclastic mood of *Cuckoo's Nest* is nostalgia, "nostalgia for a period in which the pitting of a heroic protagonist against a hostile, persecuting bourgeoisie corresponded roughly to social fact."[28]

Popular culture manifests itself in the novel in ways besides allusions to folk heroes. The Big Nurse's ward is described as having "that clean orderly movement of a cartoon comedy" (34); the patients' conversation is "like cartoon comedy speech" (23) and their world is "like a cartoon world, where the figures are flat and outlined in black, jerking through some kind of goofy story that might be real funny if it weren't for the cartoon figures being real guys" (31). The way characters grow big or small in Bromden's perspective resembles a visual technique often used in cartoons. Terry Sherwood believes the novel demonstrates a noteworthy use of popular culture in a serious novel. He points out that, as in comic strips, *Cuckoo's Nest* turns on the mythic confrontation of Good and Evil. He suggests that Bromden's transformation is like that of Freddy Freeman (he means Billy Batson) to Captain Marvel; McMurphy and Bromden are like the Lone Ranger and Tonto.[29] Kesey has a keen interest in comic books and popular culture and took them seriously before Popular Culture associations and conferences became common. At Perry Lane he talked about comic-book superheroes as the honest American myths.[30] He once said in an interview, "A single *Batman* comicbook is more honest than a whole volume of *Time* magazines."[31] Discounting the exaggeration and shock effect of this statement, we are still left with a kernel of truth about his attitude toward comic books and popular culture. They function significantly in the development of theme and characterization in *Cuckoo's Nest,* and he makes deliberate use of them (e.g., Captain Marvel and Wolfman) in *Great Notion.*

In a letter to Whitney Daly describing his pleasure at seeing his first novel in print, Kesey said, "But my book is good, and has as much integrity as I am able to muster without losing my ability to laugh, and if you've hit the one solid punch dead center they can never take that away from you." Our final consideration is, how solid and dead center is that punch? Peter Beidler has suggested one respect in which the punch scores tellingly: self-reliance. This is a quality most Americans think they have or wish they had. It has been an important theme in American literature from the beginning (Puritans, Franklin, Emerson, Thoreau, Whitman, Hemingway), and a novel that celebrates it effectively is bound to make an impact. Beidler says self-reliance "is made up in part of self-confidence (knowing that you *can*), in part of self-trust (knowing that *you* can), in part of self-consciousness (*knowing* that you can), and in part of self-control (acting on the knowledge that you can).

Those who are self-reliant are usually not bound by authority or tradition, are independent in thought, and are courageous and tenacious in pursuit of their goals."[32] Self-reliance is usually accompanied by optimism. Kesey once said he gets weary of people "who use pessimism to avoid being responsible for all the problems in our culture. A man who says, we're on the road to disaster, is seldom trying to wrench the wheel away from the driver. I prefer the troublemaker. He tells them he doesn't like the way they're running the show, that he thinks he could do better, that the fact is he's going to *try!*"[33] McMurphy has the kind of self-reliance Beidler describes, and it is precisely what the patients need. Contemporary readers want to be shown that it works, and they want to be shown that the weak can become strong, the cowardly brave, and the impotent potent: *Cuckoo's Nest* does these things.

The question remains as to how convincingly it does them. Terry Sherwood thinks the novel sentimentalizes and oversimplifies moral problems: "Kesey believes in the comic strip world in spite of himself. . . . He forgets that the comic strip world is not an answer to life, but an escape from it. The reader finds Kesey entering that world too uncritically in defense of the Good."[34] Others are disturbed by the way that self-reliance is asserted; they find it merely a matter of jokes, games, obscenity, and verbal disrespect, and doubt that throwing butter at walls, breaking windows, stealing boats, and doing what comes naturally is really the answer for achieving lasting sanity and self-esteem. They feel the novel's "yes" to life is anarchic and that too much emphasis is placed on the sexual and scatological as weapons against the impersonal and repressive aspects of society. Bruce Wallis has pointed out that it is not the Combine that generates the evil Kesey observes, but the evil that generates the Combine. The flaws in the system result from anterior flaws in the people who created and maintain it. The philosophy of the novel, in attacking the system, is attacking the symptom instead of the disease.[35]

If the message of *Cuckoo's Nest* is that emotional stability and human dignity are to be achieved simply through vulgar and anarchic rebellion against authority, then the novel has questionable worth despite its humor and its engaging battle between freedom and oppression. If its saving laughter is nothing more than defiant ridicule or irresponsible escape, then it has little to contribute to solving the puzzling but all-important question of the proper relationship between society and the individual. If Kesey believes that the answer to the dehumanizing abuse of technology is to give reign to sensual impulse, then getting back in touch with the natural world can mean little more than being close to nature the way an animal is. There is a disturbing adolescent tendency persistent in Kesey to equate the scatological with freedom, vitality, manliness, and naturalness. Perhaps it partly originated in his exposure during an impressionable period to Beat literature, life in North Beach, and the nascent counterculture of Perry Lane. It undoubtedly results partly from his rural background, the coarser elements of which he may have exaggerated as a stance toward the attractive but rather intimidating intellectual and cultural sophistication he encountered in coming to California. Whatever its source, it is apparent in *Cuckoo's Nest*. It is possible, however, to interpret the novel by viewing the obscenity as a means rather than an end. McMurphy is a coarse and vulgar personality, but the victory wrought by him is not merely a triumph of coarseness and vulgarity. His crude strength and cocky self-centeredness are manifestations in caricature of an underlying moral strength and a salutary self-respect. His example should not be taken at face value; it is symbolic on an unconventional, almost cartoon level of values that are conventional in the most positive and universal sense: self-reliance, compassion for the weak, hope, perseverance, self-sacrifice, and harmony with nature.

Chapter Three
Sometimes a Great Notion

"It's a Big Book"

Soon after completing *Cuckoo's Nest,* in June 1961, Kesey sublet the cottage in Perry Lane and returned to Oregon. During the summer he worked with his brother Chuck at the creamery. Later he moved to a summer home near Mercer Lake in the logging country of western Oregon. A friend of his parents had committed suicide and the widow wanted the house occupied. She lived in the only other house nearby and let Kesey live in the vacant house without cost so as to have a neighbor. Faye and the children did not join him for a few weeks because Zane was ill. In a letter to Babbs he describes the house as bordered on one side by the lake, "and by the impregnable, dripping green jungle of blackberry and fern and rhododendron and fir on the other." "I am here like the last human on earth holding out against the marauding wilderness that would usurp my sanity, holding out with my only weapon a typewriter." This description suggests the setting of *Sometimes a Great Notion,* the novel he began working on at this time. It is about logging, and he gathered information by accompanying the loggers into the woods by day and into the bars they frequented at nights. Since he was a native of the area, he fit in unobtrusively and carefully observed the logging business and the people involved in it. After about four months of this, he returned to Perry Lane, where most of the writing was done.

In writing his second novel, Kesey knew it would be measured by the first. He was self-conscious about not doing over again what he had done in *Cuckoo's Nest.* He was aiming at something different and more ambitious. He had experimented with narrative technique in the first novel; he would carry the experiments considerably further in the second. In many ways *Great Notion* is markedly different from *Cuckoo's*

Nest. It is significantly larger in scope as well as in number of words, technically it is more elaborate and complex, and it contains a greater range of prose style. But in theme and situation and characterization it parallels *Cuckoo's Nest* in obvious ways. Ken Babbs once made a statement that captured Kesey's imagination; he quoted it a number of times and included it in *Great Notion*: "A man should have the right to be as big as he feels it's in him to be." This is essentially the theme for both novels.

Cuckoo's Nest had taken ten months to write; he worked about two years on *Great Notion*. On one of the tapes in the Kesey Collection, he refers to it as a "dangerous" book. He says *Cuckoo's Nest* is a straightforward parable. In the second book he is treating something "vague" and "tenuous" and grappling more seriously with life-and-death questions. What did he mean by "dangerous"? Perhaps he had in mind the risks he took as a writer in trying to convey a situation comprehensively by radical manipulation of time, point of view, and narrative technique. In his notes for the novel, just after he has envisioned some of the techniques he could use, he says, "Can I do it? I'm sure I can. Mean work, but I think the work would be more fun because there would be in it the spark of danger, the tingle of experiment, the fantasy of greatness, the chance of doing something better than I could possibly do with the *best* utilization of all present methods & techniques . . . and a feeling of pure mischief and cussedness." Elsewhere in his notes, he fears he is attempting too much: "My book is trying maybe too goddamn much, trying to encompass a man, a family, a town, a country, and a time—all at once, simultaneously, and work them into a story, and have the story say something important. Awful much, Awful much."[1] And there was also the danger of addressing large issues such as life-and-death urges in relation to nature and society. It is easy to make a fool of oneself treating life-and-death questions in fiction. Kesey was particularly self-conscious about the risk he ran in treating them with his folksy, homespun approach. As he mentioned to Babbs in a letter, he was always thinking, " 'If this doesn't come off it's going to sound so corny and overwritten and sentimental that everybody will laugh their heads off at me.' I run a greater danger of this than you do, what with intellectual friends who are prone to put down the homesy and sentimental."

The intellectual friends were important to him, for he shared many of their interests. At the same time, he was shaped by a rural background, outdoor activities, and athletics. These two sides were apparent in his college years. He felt comfortable with friends engaged in writing and drama, and he felt comfortable with friends in athletics. Each set of associates wondered what he saw in the other. It was probably inevitable that the two sides of his personality would find separate expression in his fiction; this happens in *Great Notion*. To Gordon Lish's questions, "Where are you going in *Great Notion*? What is it you're testing?" Kesey answered: "For one thing, I want to find out which side of me really is: the woodsy, logger side—complete with homespun homilies and crackerbarrel corniness, a valid side of me that I like—or its opposition. The two Stamper brothers in the novel are each one of the ways I think I am."[2] *Cuckoo's Nest* is written in a vernacular idiom, an idiom obviously congenial to Kesey, and much of *Great Notion* is done in the same idiom; but one of the things he desired to do in the second novel was to try his hand at a more intellectual prose. This he did in the sections written from the younger brother's point of view, and in certain other parts of the narration.

In another letter to Babbs, Kesey said of the *Great Notion* manuscript: "It's a big book. Possibly a damned big book. Certainly a remarkable book. Perhaps even a great book. If it fails—and it could fail and still be very close to being a great book—I'll have still learned a hell of a lot about writing from doing it, enough I hope, to know better than to try anything so cumbersome again." (He was always candid with Babbs and respected his opinions enough that he sent the manuscript to Vietnam while Babbs was there.) The writing must have been a complicated project. His walls were covered with charts and diagrams of the structure and organization, and at one time he had three manuscripts in three colors lying about. The charts and diagrams were not preserved. The cottage in Perry Lane where he did most of the writing was torn down while the writing was in process, and life at La Hunta became a little chaotic about the time the novel was completed. But the notes for the novel that have been preserved provide examples of the kinds of diagraming he did. He has, in fact, not tried anything so cumbersome again. His turning from writing after *Great Notion* may have been partly a reaction to the intense effort and concentration that novel required.

Great Notion is nowhere near as widely known as *Cuckoo's Nest*. The extraordinary sales of the first novel were due largely to a young audience. The second novel did not reach the same audience. The public expected something similar to *Cuckoo's Nest* and *Great Notion* appeared very different. Reviews, although good in New York, were absent elsewhere; Kesey was not solidly established with the critics at that time. Younger people did not take to it, probably because of its size and technical complexity, and consequently there was no word-of-mouth praise, no underground rooting, as there had been with *Cuckoo's Nest*.

Likewise, the movie version did not approach the success of the Academy Award-winning version of *Cuckoo's Nest*. The actors were famous (Paul Newman, Henry Fonda, Tuesday Weld) and appropriately cast, and the novel provides an adequate and interesting story line even when the elements not reproducible by the film medium are subtracted. The weakness of the movie (later reissued with the title *Never Give an Inch*) lies primarily in the editing. Gaps in continuity mar the effect and fragment the experience.

The basic reason *Great Notion* is less popular than *Cuckoo's Nest,* even though it is in many ways the more significant novel, is that it must be read more than once and its length discourages the second reading. Many novels are rich enough to warrant multiple readings, but they probably render more upon first reading than does *Great Notion.* Its nonsequential time scheme, its multi-voiced narrative mode, and its use of various cinematic narrative devices necessitate rereading. In fact, a third reading may be needed before the many intricately developed patterns are fully understood and appreciated. The techniques are really not abstruse or obscure; there are just too many of them to take in on the first reading. Kesey had no desire to mystify or bewilder; he just wanted to include as many facets of the story—many of them subtle and subjective—as possible. Brain-wracking analysis is not necessary, but attentive rereading is.

The Story

Because of the nonsequential mode of narration, a summary of the story is useful before analysis and interpretation.

Just at the turn of the century, Jonas Stamper, a member of a "stringly-muscled brood of restless and stubborn west-walkers," comes to Oregon from Kansas, pursuing a dream of a promising new frontier.

He begins a large frame house on the banks of the Wakonda Auga River, but is soon intimidated by the country, which makes a man feel small and insignificant and is "permeated with dying." Before the house is completed, he walks out on his family and returns to Kansas. His son Henry takes charge of the family, completes the house, and begins a long struggle to keep it from being washed away by the river, which involves constantly shoring the foundation with timbers and cables. This endeavor symbolizes a struggle against death and defeat. And the struggle is carried out alone. Henry refuses to receive help from the community or to join the Wakonda Co-op. When Jonas sends from Kansas a copper bas-relief of Jesus carrying a lamb with the inscription "Blessed Are the Meek, for They Shall Inherit the Earth" as a gift at the birth of Henry's first son, Henry paints it over with yellow machine paint and prints in red, "NEVER GIVE AN INCH." He then nails it on the wall over the baby's crib.

The baby, named after his father but known as Hank, becomes just as tough and stubborn and self-reliant as his father, and he eventually takes over the task of shoring up the house against the eroding force of the river. When he is ten, his mother dies, and Henry, now fifty-one, goes to New York City for another wife. To everyone's surprise he returns with the most eligible catch available, a beautiful twenty-one-year-old, educated at Stanford, from a wealthy and fashionable family. From this union a second son is born, Leland Stanford Stamper. Apparently content with one son in his own image, Henry ignores Leland and leaves his rearing to the mother. Hank is twelve when Leland is born. When he is sixteen, his stepmother, feeling trapped, lonely, and alienated in her coarse environment, seduces him. Henry never learns of their relationship, or at least never acknowledges his awareness of it, but Leland observes them through a hole in the wall and is psychologically wounded. He develops an obsession with his brother, blended of fear, hate, and envy. When Leland is twelve, he leaves with his mother on the pretext of a vacation, but they do not return. They settle in New York, where Myra, the mother, pursues an eccentric way of life and eventually throws herself from a high building.

This background information is provided through a variety of narrative methods; the main action takes place during a matter of weeks in 1961. Hank is running the family logging business with the help of his cousin and best friend Joe Ben. Henry has been injured working in the woods and has a cast on most of one side of his body, which slows him down only a little, but he cannot work. It is a family, nonunion business. The union loggers in the area are on strike, but the Stampers have a contract with the big lumber company to supply logs. Partly because he is short-handed and partly because he feels a responsibility for his younger brother, Hank sends for Leland, who is doing graduate work in English literature at Yale. Leland is now twenty-four, his mother has recently committed suicide, and his life is a mess of drugs and paranoia. In fact, the card from Oregon arrives just as he has unsuccessfully attempted to gas himself. Without knowing exactly why but feeling a need to prove himself and get revenge upon his brother, Leland takes a bus to Oregon and goes to work in the woods with his family, waiting for an opportunity to get back at Hank. At first, but only momentarily, Henry is upset with Leland's return; he has the boy pegged as a quitter like Jonas. And, indeed, Leland embodies his grandfather's weakness and futile outlook.

The local union leader, Floyd Evenwrite, discovers the Stamper contract. Floyd has been jealous of Hank since high school and welcomes a chance to vent the anger and frustration resulting from envy of Hank's strength. He calls in Jonathan Draeger, a union leader from California, to help him. Floyd is a blustering, bumbling, impulsive, unintelligent man. Draeger is just the opposite: educated, coldly rational, confident in his knowledge of how to manipulate people. Between them they provoke the community's feelings against the Stampers.

Hank Stamper, a sort of modern western hero, becomes the focal point for a variety of pressures. He must combat the forces of nature as represented in the river constantly gnawing at the foundation of his house. With a small crew he must cut enough trees to supply a large and important contract. He must resist the social pressure exerted by the town, which gradually takes its toll among the relatives on his payroll. The pressure is intense because the people blame him not simply for their economic straits, but for a variety of personal discontents. One man even calls him to say he is going to commit suicide because of conditions produced by the Stampers' refusal to give in to the union. There is also pressure from the father he loves not to give in to the town. In addition, Hank must contend with his brother's desire for revenge, which eventually takes the form of a campaign to seduce his wife, Viv. On every hand the "never give a inch" style of his life is tested to the extreme.

The pressures reach a climax when the optimistic Joe Ben is drowned, Henry's good arm is severed in an accident and he is mortally injured, the man from town accidentally carries out his suicide threat, and Lee succeeds in seducing Viv. The cost of self-sufficient independence becomes too high for Hank and he decides to give in, but his capitulation has ironic negative effects upon the community. It becomes apparent that although everyone wanted to bring the strong man down, his giving up disillusions them and erodes their confidence in facing life. Floyd Evenwrite even engages in sabotage in order to provoke Hank to his old stubbornness.

While Lee has been scheming revenge, he has learned something about courage and the virtues of work and self-reliance and closeness with nature. In the inevitable fist-fight showdown with Hank, he is not beaten; the fight ends in a kind of draw. One result of it is that Hank decides not to give in to the union and prepares to take the logs down the river alone. Lee, who discovers that Hank had been sending money to his mother over the years and paying an insurance premium for his benefit, joins his brother on the log raft. Each of the brothers has learned something from the other. Viv, who is associated by imagery and other means with Myra, the woman at the source of the conflict between the brothers, leaves just as Hank and Lee begin the log drive. Henry has died, but Hank hangs his severed arm with all but the middle finger tied down from the house's signal pole, a defiant gesture toward the union members gathered across the river.

Narrative Techniques

Kesey told Gordon Lish that in *Great Notion* he was "fooling around with reality and what reality can be."[3] What he meant by this is revealed in the novel's attempt to express the complex subjective aspects of life. *Great Notion* aims at conveying the total reality of a primary event. This involves multiple perceptions, both objective and subjective, and it involves merging and telescoping time. The usual linear order of language is inadequate for Kesey's objective, so he tries a variety of unconventional methods. He uses not only multiple points of view but points of time. Ronald Billingsley, who has gone farthest in analyzing the novel's techniques, says Kesey is trying to achieve "spatial form": the reader is supposed to see the work "spatially in a moment of time" rather than in sequence. This description is suggestive, but not entirely satisfactory.

What really happens in the novel is that time remains fluid, and temporal arrangement is only important within small units. For the novel as a whole, temporal arrangement is subordinated to the themes and motifs and the characters and events that reveal them. Kesey is concerned with the events of a single day. His notes for the novel say, "This book, this story, is the real story of one day, one very important and particular day chosen out of many days, many months, many years. The day Hank brings the boom downriver." The events of this day epitomize the thematic issues he desires to explore. And in order for that day to have such significance, the context of setting, characters, and conflicts must be available to the reader in a comprehensiveness that includes multiple perspectives and subjective awareness transcending time. In other words, the reader must know the personality and subjective life of the main participants; he must know what the Stamper house represents and the family tradition centered there, and even the larger frontier experience that generated that tradition; and he must understand the community of Wakonda and what it represents. Of course the whole truth about even the most insignificant event can never be fully known, let alone captured in the printed words of a novel; but that does not negate the value of ambitious attempts. *Great Notion* is one of those attempts. Its strategy requires the reader to put the parts together and perceive them as a whole, to apprehend the novel as a total unit rather than as a linear sequence of events. The demands upon the reader are too much for a first reading (even though a first reading can be fascinating and enjoyable), but are justified by a second.

Billingsley compares the form of the book to a spoked wheel. The hub is the bringing of the logs downriver in defiance of the town; all other events are spokes. In his notes for the novel, Kesey says, "The book would start in the middle and grow in all directions, like a crystal." It does not really start in the middle, but rather at the end. The analogy of the crystal, however, is appropriate.

In planning the method and style, Kesey says in his notes he wanted "a cross between Faulkner and Burroughs and also me."[5] He had great admiration for Faulkner, who was a primary source of his experiments with multiple points of view and time. *Great Notion* resembles *Light in August* in the way it begins near the end and then backs up to fill in the private history of the principal characters. And its multiple points of view (Billingsley counts twelve of them) are extensions and elaborations and refinements of the techniques used in *The Sound and the Fury* and *As I Lay Dying*. Besides Faulkner and Burroughs, Kesey drew upon other writers in search of techniques for accomplishing his purposes. As he ponders in his notes how to achieve the panoramic effects he wants, he reminds himself to review *The Grapes of Wrath, John Brown's Body,* and *Under Milk Wood.*

In addition to literary models, Kesey imitated cinematic techniques. He was keenly interested in filmmaking and convinced that cinematic devices could be adapted effectively to the writing of fiction. In analyzing the ways Kesey's images are presented cinematically, Billingsley identifies such devices as "dissolve," "cross cut," "direct cut," "montage," and "flash-forward." In his notes, Kesey frequently uses such phrases as "now the camera directs toward . . ." and "the camera then cuts to. . . ." At one point in his planning, he says, "I could put it all down like a screen play practically." A characteristic device in the novel is to show simultaneous action—what various characters in various places are doing at a particular moment. As he is working out the method in his notes, he asks himself, "What does this remind me of? The narrator on Elliot Ness [the television series "The Untouchables"]; 'as so-and-so were doing *this* such-and-such was on his way into town to do this. . . .'"[6]

Kesey's notes reveal that he was trying to use as many narrative techniques as he could think of and handle. At one point he asks himself, "I have how many distinguishing forms to occur at once?" In answer he supplies this list:

> 3rd person—past
> 1st person—past
> 3rd person—present
> 1st person—present
> 2nd person? (old man talking to writer?)
> Parenthesis
> Italics

Of this list, only the second-person point of view was not incorporated into the narration. Often several of these forms appear in the same paragraph; and there is not strict division between past and present. He is trying to express the nonrational feel of experience. The novel begins on Thanksgiving Day 1961, shifts back to 1898, and then moves about freely and fluidly within that span. His notes mention "the think back within technique" that he intended to use for exposition. This is a flash-back method, unique in combining first- and third-person narration and an admixture of past and present.

To aid the reader in adapting to his multi-faceted narration, Kesey offers this advice near the beginning:

STOP! DON'T SWEAT IT. SIMPLY MOVE A FEW INCHES LEFT OR RIGHT TO GET A NEW VIEWPOINT. Look . . . Reality is greater than the sum of its parts, also a damn sight holier. And the lives of such stuff as dreams are made of may be rounded with a sleep but they are not tied neatly with a red bow. Truth doesn't run on time like a commuter train, though time may run on truth. And the Scenes Gone By and the Scenes to Come flow blending together in the sea-green deep while Now spreads in circles on the surface. So don't sweat it. For focus simply move a few inches back or forward. And once more . . . look:[7]

Later in the novel he elaborates this relation of time and reality:

Time overlaps itself. A breath breathed from a passing breeze is not the whole wind, neither is it just the last of what has passed and the first of what will come, but is more—let me see—more like a single point plucked on a single strand of a vast spider web of winds, setting the whole scene atingle. That way; it overlaps. . . . As prehistoric ferns grow from bathtub planters. As a shiny new ax, taking a swing at somebody's next year's split-level pinewood pad, bites all the way to the Civil War. As proposed highways break down through the stacked strata of centuries. (200)

These passages are important for understanding the rationale behind Kesey's experimental techniques. He was trying to capture the significant elements in events that are not revealed by the unusual objective and sequential manner of narration. Any event or feeling is related to others, and the reality of that event or feeling can be fully known only when the relationships are perceived or experienced as a simultaneous whole.

Lee gives us additional hints as to the way the novel works when he comments on modern narrative techniques and describes how he sees multiple scenes "as one scene, composed of dozens of simultaneous events." He points out that chronological reporting is not by any means the most truthful—"each camera has its own veracity." Then, with an interesting reversal of Bromden's statement in *Cuckoo's Nest,* "But it's the truth even if it didn't happen," he says. "Besides, there are some things that can't be the truth even if they *did* happen" (74). What Kesey is suggesting is that the truth he is aiming at requires multiple views, both objective and subjective, and freedom from strict sequential time.

Occasionally he tightly compresses particular times, characters, and events as a way of suggesting how the times and events of the novel as a whole should be viewed in simultaneous relation to one another: "Jonas pulls, straining at the fog. Joe Ben goes into a state park with a brush knife and an angel's face, seeking freedom. Hank crawls through a tunnel of blackberry vines, seeking thorny imprisonment. The arm twists and slowly untwists. The logger sitting in the mud calls curses across the water. 'I'm hollowed out with loneliness,' the woman cries. The water moves" (41). Here are six characters involved in events transpiring over a period from 1898 to 1961 united in the present tense—as though it were all happening right now. The development of the novel establishes the unity of these apparently disparate elements. And the mention of the moving water is important because the river, which Kesey identified with time in his notes, is a unifying presence in the book.

The introductory passage for chapter two provides another suggestive analogy for how reality can be perceived. The narrator wishes he had a pitchman to push the product, which is *"this little Wonder of the Everyday World. Tilt it, tip it, peer through it from any position . . . and your gaze you'll notice comes out someplace else. Seenow: the spheres lie concentrically one inside the other like diminishing glass balls becoming so* minute! . . . *You cannot perceive the smallest without the aid of scientific devices"* (44). His multiple narrative techniques are equivalent to tipping and tilting the glass spheres.

The novel is organized into eleven unnumbered chapters, the absence of numbers reinforcing the elimination of sequence. As a way of providing a compensating coherence for the lack of ordinary time sequence, Kesey begins each chapter with an italicized passage, usually an anecdote, that suggests a theme. This is a method especially congenial to him, for he has a natural inclination to perceive and express ideas and concepts in narrative examples— little anecdotes or parables. But, typical of the diversity of point of view in this novel, these introductory passages are not provided by exactly the same narrator. Sometimes it is Kesey speaking directly and autobiographically; sometimes it is a narrative persona, an unnamed resident of the Wakonda region. Sometimes the passages are straightforward and objective, and sometimes figurative and subjective.

Space is unavailable here to consider the many narrative devices employed in the novel. Two examples displaying notable originality will have to suffice.

The first might be called the method of convergence. It appears frequently either to introduce new points of view or events. Kesey diagramed the technique rather elaborately in his notes.[8] It was inspired by cinematic methods, as is apparent in these notes:

> Splicing? Quick glimpse of scenes to come. Quick images.
>
> We're going along when a line triggers an image in the future. The image occurs some way. Finally the scene going and the scene sneaking in mesh and the scene sneaking in takes over.
>
> Or like scenes in a morning dissolving into one another as scene gaining reaches its end we have already slipped in exposition for scene to come. Like background noise coming in over scene or background noise incongruous to *what is happening* at the moment before your eyes, but fitting with what is to happen.[9]

In these preliminary notes, he was thinking of images. By the time he did the actual writing, he had realized that the same device could be used in merging narrative points of view. He stretches this method almost too far in the fifth chapter, which includes the hunt. Molly the hound is mentioned briefly at the beginning on page 200. Similar brief mentions or images appear periodically through the chapter, but it is not until page 272 that we understand she has been bitten by a snake while chasing a bear. The gradual convergence, which arouses the reader's curiosity, serves a symbolic and thematic purpose. Hank is courageous and persistent like Molly, the bear is the pressure exerted to make him give in, and Lee's attempt at revenge is the snake clinging to him. This is an example of the convergence of events and motifs. Converging points of view are treated similarly. For example, a brief shift to Lee's point of view occurs near the end of chapter one (40), but it is not until well into the second chapter that it takes over the center of attention.

A second example demonstrates the method of simultaneous narration. Kesey often has several events unfolding at the same time. They come gradually and in fragments and are often mutually illuminating. In chapter six a Halloween day in the present is blended with one in the past. The introductory passage sets the framework with an anecdote concerning an echo canyon that will give back a phrase of song sung into it: "And even after you leave this mossy acoustical phenomenon to go on with your hiking or fishing, you cannot help feeling, for a long time after, that any jig you whistle, hymn you hum, or song you sing is somehow immutably tuned to an echo yet unheard, or relentlessly echoing a tune long forgotten—" (286). It is Lee who hears the echoes in this case. His walk through town and on the beach and his near drowning parallel the events of a childhood Halloween when he fell into a hole near the beach. The earlier experience is related in italicized sections interspersed in the action of the present. Lee's relation with Hank is the center of focus for both incidents, and in both Hank is a rescuer. This overlay of the past on the present, or simultaneous narration, effectively informs the reader of the nature and complexity of the brothers' relationship and significantly furthers the development of the main themes as they relate to both of them. And, as is characteristic of all the chapters, the unfolding of the two Halloweens is only part of the exposition going on. This same chapter includes sections on Viv, Indian Jenny, Joe Ben, the old boltcutter, Floyd Evenwrite and the union, and the fight with Big Newton. Kesey is like a juggler with many things in the air at the same time.

With his plugging in every kind of narrative technique that occurred to him, Kesey ran the risk of this experimentation becoming an end in itself. The danger of style deflecting the reader's attention away from the story is very real. Kesey was clearly aware of it. He chides himself in his notes: "I've got to get on and finish instead of constantly starting over with new wild innovations." In another place is this reminder: "I don't want to sacrifice my book to prose, character or plot—the more important thing must show through which is . . . . .? STORY."[10] In discussing his narrative techniques with Lish, he acknowledged the danger of an artist focusing on such devices to the extent of losing his sense of people: "I don't think you can veer very far from human problems and emotions and still suck the reader into turning the page. That's the writer's *first* job: suck the reader into turning the page. Otherwise, why put a ribbon in a typewriter?"[11] Once the initial shock of the nature and diversity of *Great Notion*'s narrative techniques is over, and unfortunately this might take much of a first reading to happen for many readers, the story of the Stampers is highly engaging. The characters have a depth and vitality that arouse our interest and fasten them in our memories.

The Themes

Kesey's notes for *Great Notion* are unusual.[12] He used a kind of stream of consciousness technique, recording ideas as they occurred. It is as though he were chatting with himself, making comments, criticisms, and reminders during the very process of inspiration or creation. The method derives partly from the techniques he used during the drug experiments, when he instantaneously recorded on tape or paper what was registering in his consciousness. To read the notes is often like being inside his mind watching the process of creation in its candid and unpremeditated form. Consequently, they are a fascinating revelation of how this particular novel came into being and of the process of creation in general, a remarkable opportunity to observe the genesis of fiction. And they are particularly useful in revealing the evolution of his themes.

Kesey is the kind of writer who consciously begins with themes and ideas. *Great Notion* is large and contains a diversity of characters and events, but it is thematically unified and coherent to a singular degree. Any individual thread of action or characterization will lead the perceptive reader to one of the main themes. The artistic process for Kesey consists primarily in creating characterization, events, settings, symbols, and motifs that reveal, illuminate, and establish theme. The same is true for most novelists, of course, but Kesey is among the number who rigorously insist that all elements are oriented toward theme. This approach in unskillful hands can produce idea-ridden novels in which characters mechanically and often implausibly conform to the author's thesis. The strings manipulating them are embarrassingly visible. Kesey's achievement, in both his novels, is to attain the unity and coherence and intellectual thrust provided by ideas without sacrificing vitality and apparent spontaneity in character and situation. The interpretation that follows is essentially an attempt to identify the main themes and then illustrate how they are embodied in the characters, setting, and events of the novel.

Kesey's first thinking about the novel was centered on suicide. He was interested in the connection between the Northwest's long periods of cloudy, rainy days and the rate of suicide. He learned later that in reality the suicide rate is higher during the fair weather. People somehow fight their way through the dreary season, but succumb to despair when the weather improves. His initial interests were transformed during the composition of the novel, but it retains a preoccupation with suicide and rain. The title comes from the song "Good Night, Irene" and the great notion is "To jump into the river an' drown." The opening pages call attention to the effects of the rain and damp: "The moisture. It's certainly no wonder that this area has two or three natives a month take that one-way dip—it's either drown your blasted self or rot" (2–3). This seems to reflect Kesey's original conception of the relation between rain and suicide. Later in the book, however, through the point of view of Teddy the bartender, we learn that although rain generates fear within the people of Wakonda, it is an unseasonable period of sunshine that produces "absolute, unspeakable, supreme terror" (572). The terror, of course, actually arises from Hank's apparent capitulation at this point, which, ironically, damages community morale; but Kesey deliberately conjoins it with sunshine. As the little boy in the playground announces, the sun has come out "Because that sonofabitchin' Hank Stamper is *fine-a-lee* called off his deal with Wakonda Pacific" (530). This use of sunshine conforms with Kesey's learning the actual relation between weather and depression.

Suicide and particularly drowning are important motifs. Myra commits suicide; Lee attempts it overtly with gas and more gradually through his moral and psychological weakness; Willard Eggleston contemplates it; Ray, the musician, tries it; and the death of Joe Ben's father is portrayed as a kind of suicide. The drowning motif appears throughout. Jonas deserts his family because he feels he is drowning in the wet climate (24). Hank begins his grudge match with the river when his bobcat kittens are drowned (108–9). Omar the squirrel in the anecdote that sets the theme for chapter four is drowned in a fall shower (148). Les Gibbons wishes the whole Stamper brood "was drownt" (218). Lee nearly drowns in his encounter with the teenage toughs (312–13). Joe Ben drowns—but does so laughing (511). And at the end the stepbrothers risk drowning as they take the log booms down river. These examples of suicide and drowning are given significance by the section on the deer found swimming out to sea. When it is brought in, it swims out again. As Henry and Lee discuss this phenomenon, Henry says fishermen often find animals swimming out to sea and emphasizes that it is not simply a matter of drowning: "But they wasn't just drowning; they was swimming" (254). Lee is puzzled by this until he makes the connection with his own psychological state. The point of the section is to emphasize that suicide and drowning are forms of weakness and giving up. They represent the opposite of the values Hank embodies. This is why Hank is portrayed as a champion swimmer. He used to practice by swimming against the current of the river; and he is able to swim the river even at the nadir of his strength when his best friend has just died, his father is mortally injured, there seems no way to meet the contract, and he has just been beaten up.

In some early jottings for the novel, we can see how the river-ocean-drowning images took shape in Kesey's mind:

The river flows out to sea.

The sea is surrender. Not the sea itself. No, it is a conqueror; it is the giving in to it that is surrender. It waits. It doesn't wait. It tears at the land, at life of mankind. It gnaws away our coast lives and smooths out our mountains.

The sea is always after you. The rains tear building away.

The water is death. Not dead, death.

To jump into the river is to submit to death, to watery nothingness.

The Union. The answer, yet not the answer. The labor Union is like the sea, the river: it, to the father, is surrender, death.

> The loss of identity in a great amorphous.
> Which is what drowning in the sea is.[13]

Elsewhere in the notes we find this related passage: "Hank remembers swimming with the current, floating, being swept to sea, the lulling, sleepy rocking feeling of lying on a tube floating down to Wakonda. Falling asleep and almost being washed to sea. That is what has happened to the lives of these two old buddies of his. They have given up, they are just floating to the sea, to death. Because it is easier to die than to live; it always has been. . . . You have to fight for life and freedom and individuality and then fight to keep it."[14] These notes encapsulate the principal elements of the book's central themes. They also reveal the significance of setting. Kesey has combined the river, the ocean, and the forest with its thick, moist undergrowth into a setting that reverberates as a living presence. One is reminded of the way the heath functions in Hardy's novels. It was a fortunate inspiration because the setting is not only integral to the themes, but gives the novel an almost cosmic dimension by joining elemental forces of nature with human struggle in a persuasive symbolic relationship.

The river is a rich symbol because, in addition to the eroding figurative implications already noted, it suggests the eroding effects of time. Kesey mentions this in his notes, and the first page of the novel itself describes the river as "hiding the cruel file-edge of its current beneath a smooth and calm-seeming surface." The river, like time, produces change. It has eliminated the houses along its bank—except for the Stamper place, which is a kind of anachronism, a holdout against time: "It stands as a monument to a piece of extinct geography, marking the place where the river's bank once held" (4). And of course the house represents the people who live in it, a family of wildcat loggers clinging to old-fashioned values of frontier independence. Henry and Hank obstinately resist the effects of time and aging the way the house resists the eroding pull of the river.

The novel's main concern is with the nature of strength and weakness, and the conflicts are between kinds of strength and kinds of weakness. This is apparent in the relationships between Hank and his community, between Hank and Draeger, between Hank and Lee, and between Henry and Boney Stokes. And it is true for the psychological struggles within the characters, particularly in the case of Lee.

As in *Cuckoo's Nest,* the principal value is self-reliance. Lee, like Bromden, is psychologically disturbed because his self-esteem has been undermined by family relationships in which the mother has played a key role. Hank, like McMurphy, is strong and independent, capable of helping the weak confront fear by his example of stubborn perseverance. Draeger, like Nurse Ratched, represents the rational manipulation of human beings by exploiting their fear. Both novels convey the message that the individual must come to terms with himself and eliminate self-deceiving phantasms before he can establish a satisfactory relationship with society. *Cuckoo's Nest* makes clear that life is dangerous for the strong and entails obligation toward the weak. *Great Notion* probes deeper into the challenges and burdens of being strong and self-reliant and explores more fully the psychology of weakness.

Hank

Hank Stamper is the product of a frontier culture. When Draeger goes to Viv in search of an explanation for Hank's stubborn determination to deliver the logs, she tells him there are reasons going back two or three hundred years. Draeger is not disposed to believe that the past has such a powerful shaping influence on the ways of men in the present, but this is one of his limitations. He represents the rationalistic desire for a world rendered simple, precise, and predictable. The influences shaping Hank are complex and often beyond the ken of rationalism. The reasons Viv alludes to are revealed in the section on the family history. Kesey clearly wishes to link Hank with the western American tradition. Throughout the novel Hank is associated with stock phrases from western movies;" one of the ten toughest hombres this side of the Rockies," "shootout at the OK corral," "this town isn't big enough for the both of us." The casting of Hank in the mold of the cowboy hero reveals Kesey's respect for the values embodied in western myths and gives the book a significant historical-cultural dimension. Hank becomes symbolic of a pattern of distinctively American values that seem threatened to be eclipsed by the values of a technological, collectivist society. Hank was the first of the Stampers to complete the full circle west. He had gone to Korea as a soldier: "West, west, sailing out of San Francisco west and after two years landing on the Eastern Seaboard, where his ancestors had first set foot." Hank realizes upon his return that the frontier is gone and senses a "national malady" resulting from that fact. He had expected the boys out West, his old friends, to have "style and grit," but "they acted tired, scared, asleep" (157–58). Viewed from the large perspective of the American experience, Hank represents a last stand for the independent, self-reliant perseverance characteristic of frontier values.

Hank lives out the motto on the plaque that his father nailed over his crib—"Never give a inch"—and he shares with his father the attitude that "If we don't get him this round, we'll get him the next" (192, 238). These attitudes make him a winner in athletics and a forceful contender in any struggle or competition. In one of his notes, Kesey says Hank knows that to stop fighting means to start dying. A significant event in his development is the incident in which he triumphs over fear in acquiring three bobcat kittens, only to have them swept away by the river. His battle against the river begins at this point, and it transcends the matter of the bobcats. Fighting against the river symbolizes resisting all the forces that erode freedom and the will to live. A part of Hank's will to live is his vital response to simple pleasures of the senses—milking a cow, watching the sun set after a day of work. Kesey uses a device he calls "Hank's bell" to symbolize this vitality.

The vitality can make life interesting and satisfying, but being strong entails for Hank certain burdensome consequences. He must contend with what Kesey mentions in his notes as "the pressure of the meek, striving to inherit the earth."[15] Remember that underneath the "never give a inch" motto is "Blessed are the meek, for they shall inherit the earth." The pressure from the meek comes in their desire to see the strong defeated; this confirms and justifies their meekness. Lee identifies himself at one point with Les Gibbons, a Stamper neighbor who requests favors while at the same time wishing Hank ill: "We wanted the champ down simply because it was insupportable to us that he had the audacity to be *up* there—perched arrogantly on the throne when we were not" (197).

Moreover, the weak blame their problems on the strong. An important aspect of theme is the notion of phantasms. The weak, in order to cope with guilt and frustration, attribute bad motives to the strong and blame them for their problems and unhappiness. Lee is the principal example; his paranoid phantasms prevent him from understanding Hank. They approach meaningful communication several times before the climax of the novel, but each time Lee's phantasms prevent it. The townspeople are like Lee in their blaming Hank for their personal troubles. This is one of many parallel situations in the novel. When Kesey abandoned sequential time, he needed something else to provide unity and cohesion. The method of parallels is one of the primary replacements. The townspeoples' phantasms are combined with Lee's to establish the nature of weakness and the pressures upon the strong. Two headquarters constitute the poles of the conflict between strength and weakness: the Stamper house and the Snag. At the house work is going on and Hank is shoring his foundation against the drift toward death. At the Snag is fear, inaction, and cowardly blaming.

Another burden of being strong is that Hank must prove himself with challengers. Like a cowboy with a reputation for being quick on the draw, he is obliged to take on all comers who wish to make a name for themselves by defeating him. He confronts such situations with a tired resignation; he knows they are inevitable. In the case of Tommy Osterhaust, the new challenger at high school, Joe Ben explicitly draws the comparison with westerns and says Hank must fight "on account of that's his place, no matter how he don't like it" (324). The Tommy incident is a parallel for the more central contest between Hank and Big Newton. And these encounters, whether with Tommy or Floyd Evenwrite or Big Newton, are symbolic of larger encounters, such as that with the river, in which Hank as representative of the will to live is pitted against the temptation to give in to death. As Hank says to himself in squaring off against Big at the Snag, *"I ain't running out to sea from him, I don't give a shit how big he is: he can whip my ass but he can't run me out to sea!"* (340). Hank wants Lee to be with him for this encounter because he would have Lee learn that one must fight in order to resist the enticement of giving in to the sea. They have just come from the beach where Lee has nearly allowed himself to drown. Lee cannot understand why Hank wants to face the town now that they know of his contract with Wakonda Pacific. He says "that's as good a way as any to get dead." Hank thinks to himself, "it's as good a way as any to stay alive" (322). This reveals what separates them: Hank confronts problems head on as a way of affirming life; Lee runs from them toward death.

Hank's type of self-reliant strength has other drawbacks. It inhibits his ability to communicate love and tenderness. He admits, "I've always had a tough time trying to talk to others without barking" (179). Because he refuses to lower his guard or make himself vulnerable in any way, he is shut off from certain important forms of interpersonal communion. With Henry and Joe Ben this is not a problem; they have their own rough ways to express mutual respect and regard. But it is a problem with Viv and Lee. Viv has a pressing need to help and comfort, but it is frustrated by Hank's refusal to admit pain or need. Lee is sensitive and articulate. His need is to express and analyze his hurt, but Hank's tough exterior intimidates him and consequently arouses his hostility.

Hank cannot communicate with Lee, but of course this is only a part of what separates them. The real barrier is their radically different responses to life and particularly the issue of personal strength. In pondering why he and Lee cannot get along, Hank decides it is because they have not fought—physically slugged it out. He explains to Joe Ben that the problem between him and Lee is "That we *didn't* fight. That he *won't,* and I know it and he knows it. Maybe that right there is the thing keeps us just like oil and water." Hank cannot understand or accept Lee's defeatist attitude: "But even when he knows he ain't gonna get whipped, he acts like he knows he can't win *neither*. . . . He acts like . . . he don't have any reason, ever any reason, to fight" (271). Their reconciliation comes only after their fist fight near the end of the novel.

The test of Hank's strength and determination is the center of the story, the source of tension and suspense. In Kesey's papers are two 3″ × 5″ cards; one says, "Try to make Hank give up," the other, "Wipe that goddam grin off Hank's face!" Apparently these were tacked to his wall during the process of composition. One page of his notes lists the pressures brought to bear to cause Hank to give in: "The fight against the union. The pressure from the town he loves. The pressure from the father he loves not to give in to the town. The pressure of the river. The pressure of a big workload. Finally, the losing of his wife and of Joe Ben, his best buddy." As these pressures build to a climax, the most telling of them all is that exerted by Lee. By providing an example of how one can win by being weak, Lee undermines Hank's confidence in strength. Hank says, "Yet it took nothing more than my kid brother coming to spend a month with us to show me that there are *other* ways of winning—like winning by giving in, by being soft, by not gritting your goddam teeth and getting your best hold . . . winning by not, for *damned* sure, being one of the Ten Toughest Hombres west of the Rockies. And show me as well that there's times when the only way you can win is by being weak, by losing, by doing your worst instead of your best. And learning that come near to doing me in" (111). The brothers learn something from each other. Hank's is a dangerous lesson because in learning the nature of true strength he nearly loses confidence in strength altogether. When he has decided to give in, he says to himself, "There ain't really any true strength . . . No, not the strength I always believed in . . . not strength like I always thought, I could build and thought I could live, and thought I could show the kid how to live. . . . But if the strength ain't real . . . then the weakness sure enough is. Weakness is true and real. . . . No, you can't ever fake being weak. You can only fake being strong" (523, 527). He thinks that instead of teaching Lee, he has been taught by him. This is only partially true. When he fights with Lee, and Lee for the first time fights back at something, Hank realizes that the kind of strength he wanted to teach Lee is valuable and Lee has adopted it. Seeing Lee, who he thought had succeeded through weakness, converted to the importance of strength, Hank's faith in strength is restored, but within a new perspective.

Hank needs to understand the nature and limitations of the strength he possesses; Lee provides that understanding. But Lee needs the strength itself, as does the entire town, and Hank provides the model for them. Near the end, Lee articulates this process of mutual enlightenment and confirms the value of the proper kind of self-reliant strength:

For there is always a sanctuary more, a door that can never be forced, whatever the force, a last stronghold that can never be taken, whatever the attack; your vote can be taken, your name, your innards, even your life, but that last stronghold can only be surrendered. And to surrender it for any reason other than love is to surrender love. Hank had always known this without knowing it, and by making him doubt it briefly I made it possible for both of us to discover it. I knew it now. And I knew that to win my love, my life, I would have to win back for myself the right to this last stronghold.

Which meant winning back the strength I had bartered away years before for a watered-down love. (622–23)

The moral core of the novel is the sanctity of this last stronghold. To surrender it without just cause is the way of weakness and produces a life of fear, envy, and despair. To refuse surrender for any cause, even love, is likewise damaging and produces a life of lonely alienation.

Hank's vitality is composed in large measure of animal strength. It is a robustness of the outdoors, a man who works in the forest with his hands. It is appropriate, therefore, that Kesey symbolically reinforces Hank's situation by using animals: the dog and the goose. Both serve a figurative purpose in *Cuckoo's Nest* as well. Molly the hound, who pursues the bear alone while the rest of the pack follows easier game, is a parallel for Hank, and the snake that bites her corresponds to Lee's scheme for revenge. The geese in chapter eight are used to accentuate Hank's inner conflict as he approaches the climactic struggle with the pressures exerted upon him. He has always had an affinity for the geese; their call evokes a complex and powerful feeling within him, and he does not like to see them killed. The sound of the geese represents independence and the "grit and style" he admires. This sound is pulling him in one direction and the sound of the phone, representing pressure from the community, the temptation to give in, is pulling him in the other. As the tension mounts, he says he is as tired of the geese as he is of the people and wishes "they would *all* shut up *altogether*" (422). He identifies with a lone goose, whose situation parallels his own disorientation: "he wasn't so much just asking where the lost flock was—he was wanting to know where the river was, and the bank, and *everything* hooked up with his life. *Where is my world?* he was wanting to know, *and where the hell am I if I can't locate it?* He had lost his way and was out there flying the river, out of his head looking for it" (443). He prevents Joe Ben from shooting a lone goose; but later, when he is weakening, he takes a shotgun himself. When he finally decides to ease up and let someone else take over, the sound of the geese stops, "and the hole left in the night by their honking was like a big roaring vacuum; enough to wake anybody" (469). Immediately after the geese sound is silenced, Hank is startled by his own reflection and he fails to do his usual securing of the foundation of the house—obvious signs of weakness. In addition to embodying animal vitality and physical strength, Hank also represents a kind of idealism. His obstinacy is employed in maintaining a set of old-fashioned values. This theme of idealism is subtly augmented by a pair of contrasting parallels. The stories of Simone and Indian Jenny seem at first only tangentially related to the central conflict, and readers are puzzled by the fact that the last lines of the book—an obvious place of emphasis—are devoted to Jenny. Simone serves as an example of idealism betrayed. She may be kidding herself in having men and religious scruples simultaneously, but even an ideal based on self-deception can be better than none. After forsaking her principles, she enters the Snag just as Jenny leaves: "Simone, resigned and irreligious in lascivious scarlet, whisks in the same door, and surrenders the sweet-cake naïveté in her heart forever" (572). The humor in this surrender is tinged with sadness. Later, we see her putting away her statue of the Virgin: "Could a virgin be expected to understand safety jelly? or Listerine gargle? or the cold cyst that swelled like a frozen bubble beneath her skin, the cold, hollow left when you for now and evermore relinquish Virtue, and Contrition, and even Shame?" (580). She has given in, and her capitulation strategically coincides with Hank's temporary surrender. Jenny, on the other hand, who leaves the Snag as Simone enters, does not give up. Her ideal is a love for the image of Henry in his youth. She tries every kind of magic to possess that image and repeatedly vows, "I ain't giving up." She is "tenacious" and "resolute" and in the end succeeds. She resists time the way Hank and Henry do. The Jenny-Henry motif is played off against the town-Hank relationship. Henry had insulted Jenny but "the image of a green-eyed, proud-eyed young logger with a bristling mustache will not let her sleep" (544). Likewise, the town is indignant with Hank's arrogant, independent behavior but cannot do without it.

The fact that Wakonda needs Hank's defiance is important. It signifies that without obstacles and challenges human life loses meaning. As Big Newton puts it, "Dammit anyhow. . . . What does a guy *do* . . . when his purpose in life peters out?" (539). A certain amount of resistance is necessary to prod people into mustering and exerting the best that is in them. Even the Wakonda High School football team plays better when they have Hank to hate; and Floyd misses Hank's opposition enough that he commits arson in order to provoke him to his old defiance. Furthermore, it indicates that strong individuals are needed to generate confidence in those lacking strength. The people in the Snag are frightened and discontent while Hank refuses to give in, but their fear and discontent are greatly magnified when he does. As much as they blame and curse him, he still provides for them necessary evidence that a self-reliant will to live is possible and counts for something. If someone like Hank cannot give an inch, then it is possible for them to resist at least to a meaningful degree.

Lee

In his portrayal of Hank, Kesey explores the nature of strength—its values, obligations, and costs. His portrayal of Lee explores the nature of weakness—its sources, manifestations, and consequences.

One of the challenges Kesey consciously took upon himself in doing this novel was to create an intellectual character and write in his idiom. He had proved his artistry in the vernacular in *Cuckoo's Nest*; now he wanted to do intellectual prose. The contrasting brothers should have contrasting idioms and habits of mind. Besides using grammar and diction to establish these contrasts, Kesey relies heavily upon similes and literary allusions. The similes Hank frequently uses, or those the narrator uses in describing him, are of a vernacular sort: "like the plucked wings of a muscle-bound stewing chicken sneaking way across the kitchen floor behind the chef's back"; "people all know where the bone is buried now"; "like a dog shitting peach pits." Lee's similes have a literary or educated flavor: "which Henry relinquished with about as much enthusiasm as Napoleon must have shown giving up his sword on the isle of Saint Helena"; "with the air of a dandy adjusting his foulard." Lee's narration is filled with literary allusions, reflecting his literary studies at Yale.

These devices of language help establish the contrast between the two, but Kesey goes further. The differences between the brothers are seen from the inside as well as the outside. With his technique of multiple points of view, Kesey demonstrates how differently the two minds work. The omniscient narrator describes the brothers; other characters, notably Joe Ben, describe them; they describe each other; and each reveals himself from both an objective and a more subjective first-person point of view. As a result, the reader has a clear and comprehensive impression of what separates the two and consequently understands and is engaged by the conflict.

When Lee returns to Oregon, his life is a mess. He has lost hope in the future; he has attempted suicide; he is paranoid and has been under analysis; he is irresponsible; he is using drugs; he is broke; he fears he is impotent; and he has allowed his physical condition to deteriorate. He needs help the way Bromden does at the beginning of *Cuckoo's Nest*. Both experience paranoid phantasms. Lee's analyst tells him many of the disturbed of his generation have a talent for releasing frustration through clever fantasy. "And you, you are the worst of the lot on that score" (71). Kesey mentioned in his notes that he wanted something for Lee comparable to Bromden's Combine. What he came up with was "Old Reliable," which Lee characterizes as "The Sentry of my Besieged Psyche" (427). This is the inner voice that repeatedly warns him to WATCH OUT. Lee trusts this alarm system completely, but of course it is in reality untrustworthy, being nothing more than the voice of fear and paranoia. It sounds the alarm at phantasms rather than at genuine dangers. When Lee was a child, Hank had told him about encountering a "Hide-behind" in the woods. This was a creature that moves so fast it is always behind a man no matter how quickly he turns to see it. On the day Lee returns, Hank thinks, "He looks like this time it's *him* that suspects a Hide-behind after him . . ." (115). As much as Lee trusts Old Reliable, it is only good for warning of Hide-behinds.

Old Reliable is actually Lee's worst enemy, the principal obstacle in the way of his finding himself and being reconciled with his brother. When Hank does something as innocuous as pointing out the beauty of a sunset, Old Reliable shouts, "WATCH OUT." It is the same when Hank tries to communicate to him his deep feelings about logging with the description of rigging the spar. Old Reliable causes him to attribute bad motives to Hank. This is the pattern throughout. Lee cannot open himself to domestic warmth and love because his warning voice convinces him these are traps. As he lies in his bed one night, his phantasms parade across the ceiling above his head: "a panorama of unparalleled paranoia, as every neuron cowered in terror from its neighbor while the sheep were being slaughtered. WATCH OUT WATCH OUT WATCH . . ." (199). He even suspects Hank's generosity: "He's being nice for some sneaky reason; beware!" (205). Hank wants Lee to accompany him to the Snag when he fights Big Newton. He has no clear reason why Lee's presence is important to him: "Maybe because the kid needed to see first-hand what kind of world was going on around his head all the time without him ever seeing it, the *real* world with *real* hassles, not this fairybook world of his that he was having most of the time like a kind of *nightmare* that him and his kind'd made up to scare theirselfs with" (334). But Lee's inner monitor causes him to misunderstand the entire situation. At first he thinks Hank is going to beat him up in front of the town, and then, after witnessing Hank's victory over Big Newton, he thinks Hank did it just as a warning for what he would do to him. This cowardly, self-centered projection of evil motives upon Hank is paralleled in the behavior of the townspeople. Floyd Evenwrite, for example, blames everything from his flat tire to his diarrhea on Hank. This is a primary characteristic of the kind of weakness at the opposite pole from self-reliant strength. The self-sufficient person has no need to project blame upon others or create phantasms to alleviate frustrations. Hank, for example, has good cause to attribute bad motives to others, but his typical response is, "Oh, well; they didn't really mean anything by it" (83).

The turning point for Lee is when he can deny Old Reliable. It comes during the fist fight with Hank. "HE'LL KILL YOU, Old Reliable kept screeching. LIE DOWN! . . . And the voice, for the first time in a long, long reign over my psyche, met with opposition. 'No,' said a stranger in my head. 'Not so' " (615). This turning point is not only the key event for Lee, it also changes Hank's mind about giving in. This is where they both come to understand the "last stronghold."

Lee's problems began in his childhood. His father paid little attention to him. "Where he had insisted on raising his firstborn to be as strong and self-sufficient as himself, he was content to let this second child—a large-eyed kid with his mother's pale skin and a look like his veins ran skim milk—spent his youth alone in a room next to his mother's doing what-the-hell-ever it was that sort of kid does alone in his room all day" (35). Consequently, he never fit in in the rough logging household; but Hank was always there as a reminder of what it meant to fit in and excel in physical activities. He had the same problem in the small logging town school, where recognition and esteem were earned on the playground rather than in the classroom. Lee "had received straight A's in everything but recess" (489). Hank, on the other hand, was the outstanding athlete in several sports. So Lee grows up feeling so smothered by Hank that he sees no reason in trying to breathe. He feels that unless he can just once best Hank in some way, he will never be able to breathe. As he tries to explain to Viv, "When I lived here, as a child, I thought Hank was the biggest thing created. I thought he knew everything, was everything, *had* everything in this whole water logged world . . . except one particular thing that was mine" (263).

That one particular thing was his mother and the sense of self-worth having her meant. Since his father ignored him, his mother became doubly important. When he discovered Hank and his mother engaged in sexual intercourse, he felt robbed of everything. The situation begs for Freudian interpretation, but Lee himself warns us against simplistic psychological symbolism:

Certainly there were all the run-of-the-mill Freudian reasons beneath my animosity toward my dear brother, all the castration-complex reasons, all the mother-son-father reasons—and all especially deep-seated and strong within me because the usual abysmal longing of the sulky son wishing to do in the guy who had been diddling Mom were in me compounded by the malevolent memories of a psychotic sibling . . . oh yes, I had numerous scenes working on these multi-faceted levels—and any one of these note-pad facts would have constituted reason enough to provoke vengeance in the heart of any loyal neurotic—but this wasn't the Whole Truth. (195)

In addition to these reasons, Hank epitomizes the most dangerous sort of man to Lee's kind of world. In Lee's eyes he is "crass, bigoted, wrongheaded, hypocritical" and substitutes "viscera for reason" and confuses "his balls with his brains" (195). But still, he says, this isn't the Whole Truth. What is the Whole Truth? The following pages reveal it. It is the natural desire of the weak that the strong should fail. Lee identifies himself with Les Gibbons—in other words with the envious townspeople—in wishing to see the champ brought down. As intriguing as the inviting Freudian implications in the novel are, Kesey's real interest is in strength and weakness and the relationships between them.

Lee's development is a process of gaining enough self-sufficiency that he can overcome fear and phantasms. He must learn not to affix blame on others (the chief characteristic of weakness in this novel): "It was my brother Hank; it was my ancient fossil of a father, who frightened and disgusted me; it was my mother, whose name be frailty . . . *they* were the ones who tore my young life asunder!" (227). He will never adopt Hank's crassness and bigotry, but at the center of Hank's character is a strength and integrity that he must learn to emulate.

As he did in *Cuckoo's Nest,* Kesey draws upon motifs from popular culture in order to enhance the texture of Lee's conflict and development. Captain Marvel and Wolfman are by far the most important. Both involve the transformation from weakness to strength or meekness to power. They are played off against each other as a means of showing Lee's ambiguous feelings about transformation. In his eyes Hank is both a Captain Marvel and a Wolfman. He envies the noble element in Hank's strength, the one corresponding to Captain Marvel, but he mistrusts the elements of brute power and animal vitality that correspond to the Wolfman.

When Lee discovers a box of old comic books in his room, he begins thinking about his "one great hero, Captain Marvel, still head and shoulders above such late starters as Hamlet or Homer." Then it occurs to him that "maybe it *wasn't* really Captain Marvel that was my hero; maybe it was Billy Batson and his magic word. I always used to try to figure out what *my* word was, *my* magic phrase that would turn me instantly enormous and invulnerable. . . . In fact, wasn't that perhaps what I was still searching for? *My* magic word?" (142–43). He feels that Hank has found his magic word, and as he searches for his during the course of the story, two options occur to him. One comes when he is responding positively to life in the Stamper family and particularly to Viv's cooking: "All those years barking Shazams up the wrong tree— you'd think a foxy kid like me woulda known better. Magic words are too hard to come by, too tricky to pronounce, too unpredictable. Steady proper diet is the secret to growth. It *has* to be. I should have learned long ago. A sweet disposition, easy-going digestion, the proper diet, and love thy neighbor as thy brother and thy brother as thyself. 'I'll do it!' I decided—'Love him as myself . . .'" (228–29). He is on the right track here, but Old Reliable speaks up to poison him toward Hank. The second option, and the one he chooses, comes from a realization that he has been saying the wrong Shazam and seeking lightning from the wrong source. Instead of seeking the usual kind of strength, he decides to use weakness as a weapon. By exploiting Viv's need to be needed, he seduces her and gets his revenge on Hank. Hank witnesses the act through the same peephole Lee had used to watch Hank and his mother—another of the novel's many parallels. Lee's first words to Hank after this has happened are described as his magic words. He begins the phrase to Hank and completes it to the doctor, tauntingly using Hank's own idiom: "Well, brother, musta been somethin' gawd-awful rich to make you so gawdawful sick." He finishes the phrase "like Billy Batson, gag ripped from his mouth, finishing the last half of a broken 'Shazam!'" But it takes only a short time for him to realize that magic words are not the answer and that his victory is an empty one: "I had very successfully completed my ritual of vengeance: I had accurately mouthed all the right mystical words . . . but instead of turning myself into Captain Marvel, as the ritual and words were supposed to do according to all the little-guy-beats-big-guy tradition . . . I had merely created another Billy Batson" (527–28). His empty victory parallels that of Floyd Evenwrite and the community.

The werewolf motif is conjoined with the Captain Marvel motif at a point where Lee turns his thoughts from what he is going to change into and reflects upon his past: "Even werewolves and Captain Marvel had a childhood didn't they" (227). But it appears most frequently in the Halloween section.

The important parallel narratives in chapter six serve not only to explain the brothers' relationship, they also reveal an important stage in Lee's development. By returning to the scene of a childhood trauma involving Hank, Lee is attempting to purge himself of some of his obsessions. Hank senses this when he says, "I can't shake this nagging notion that he'd come to the ocean for the same reason he was headed across the dunes as a kid, and I maybe had something to do with it this time too" (321). In both the childhood experience of falling down a devil's stovepipe and the present experience of nearly being drowned by the gang of teenage toughs, Hank is rescuer; but in the latter case he does not actually pull Lee out. He drives the teenagers away and then stands with his hands in his pockets, and Lee crawls out on his own. This incident is a middle stage between the childhood one, when he relied totally on Hank, and the fight at the end, when he is completely self-sufficient: "This time he had fought with nobody to pull him out from under what he knew was maybe death when he crawled under it . . . nobody to pull him out but himself" (616). He explains to Viv what happened during the fight in this way: "I was fighting for my life. I know it. Not running for my life as I've always done before. But fighting for it. Not to keep it, or to have it, but *for it* . . . fighting to get it, to *win* it" (622). When he decides to join Hank on the log boom, he begins the fight to keep it.

The Supporting Cast

The conflict between the Stamper brothers, which is the central concern, is augmented and illuminated by the other characters, all of whom are linked to it in some measure.

Viv's is an instrumental role. She is pointedly identified with Myra. Both are described with the generous use of bird imagery; both are unhappy at the Stamper house, Myra considerably more than Viv; both hunger for books and culture; both are observed in illicit sexual intercourse through the same peephole; both are love objects for both of the brothers; and so on. The brothers unconsciously make the identification. Hank insists that Viv wear her hair long, as Myra did, and he wonders what it would look like black, as Myra's was. Lee finds a picture in the attic that he thinks is of Viv and takes it with him for that reason. In reality it is a picture of Myra. Viv finally realizes the kind of surrogate role she has been playing and leaves to find a new life for herself.

Henry serves to establish the never-give-an-inch theme. He is the link with the pioneer past and the determined individualism that characterized its achievements, and his yarns are a continuation of a frontier tradition. As E. D. Webber points out, Henry and his family accurately represent the wildcat loggers of the Pacific Northwest. They are fiercely independent, often ruthless, and a little crazy. They prefer to work alone, are prone to be antisocial, and are a dying breed. The large companies and the establishment of national parks and forests are driving them out of business. "Much like the Mountain men of the 1840's, they were important if not necessary for establishing society west of the Rockies, but once society was actually established they were a definite threat. Organized society will not have wildcatters or mountain men any more than Aunt Sally will have Huck the way he is."[16] Henry's conflict with Boney Stokes is, of course, a harmonic enlargement of Hank's defiance of the community. The old boltcutter mentioned throughout the novel, who dies at the time of Henry's fatal accident, serves as a contrasting parallel. The boltcutter has Henry's independent views and was also a skilled logger in the old days, but he turns to wine, whereas Henry continues to try to "whup it." "In Oregon you got to keep on the jump," he says, "to put the hair on your chest an' keep the moss off your *rump*" (208). Hank's advice to Lee as they begin the log run is "Keep on the bounce" (627); obviously, the spirit of old Henry lives on.

Just as Hank loves Henry for his know-how, independence, and obstinate spunk, he loves Joe Ben for his vitality and optimism. The three constitute a special blending. This is clear in their work just before the accident: ". . . the three of them meshed, dovetailed . . . into one of the rare and beautiful units of effort sometimes seen when a jazz group is making it completely, or when a home-town basketball squad, already playing over its head, begins to rally to overtake a superior opponent in a game's last minute. . . . But to become this kind of perfect group a team must use *all* its components, and use them in the slots best suited, and use them all with the pitiless dedication to victory that drives them up to their absolute peak and past it" (498). This passage encapsulates some of the principal values conveyed in the novel. Kesey implies that this kind of teamwork is preferable to the collective action of unions, which often kills individual initiative. Joe Ben's death is part of the river-drowning motif, but, significantly, he laughs in the confrontation with death, thus providing a contrast to those who despairingly give in to the river and ocean. His function in the novel is symbolized by the time he spends making repairs on the Stamper house. Hank shores the foundation and fights the river; Joe Ben maintains or preserves what is won in that struggle. It is an act of gratitude. Contrast the people of the community, who also benefit from Hank's resistance to what the river represents, but who are inactive and ungrateful.

Draeger and Evenwrite are foils for Hank, and are also reverse duplications of Lee and Hank. Draeger, like Lee, is an intellectual with a background of straight A's; but, unlike Lee, he is strong. Rather than fearing people, he confidently manipulates them. Floyd comes from the same background as Hank and speaks the same idiom, but he is weak. He is committed to the union and has the model of a union father the way Hank is committed to self-reliance and has the model of his independent father. Floyd tries to impress others and worries about their opinion of him; Hank is indifferent to what others think of him.

Draeger, whose voice is described at various times as "sterile," "placid," "pure and tasteless as rainwater," and "almost mesmerizing," represents cold, manipulative rationalism. He "enjoys thinking of himself as mild-mannered and under control" (10). Like Nurse Ratched, he knows how to exploit love and fear for his purposes. "Love—and all its complicated ramifications, Draeger believed—actually does conquer all; Love—or the Fear of Not Having It, or the Worry about Not Having Enough of It, or the Terror of Losing It—certainly does conquer all. To Draeger this knowledge was a weapon" (10). The main reason for the section narrated from the point of view of Teddy, the proprietor of the Snag, is to provide a perspective on Draeger's methods and the responses of the community. Teddy admires him as a "Force" that can create fear. He is part of a spectrum of fear in the novel. There are those who succumb to it (a number of the townspeople and Lee until the end); Teddy, who has learned to escape it (with the help of his neon lights); Draeger, who uses it as a tool; and those like Hank, Joe Ben, and Henry, who have overcome it. Draeger does not believe in strong men. "The hardest man," he writes in his notebook, "is but a shell" (86). Consequently, Hank surprises and bewilders him.

Evaluation

One can go much further in relating the parts of this novel to the whole. Without being overly ingenious it is possible to relate each character and incident to the main themes. *Sometimes a Great Notion* is a large novel, but it contains little fat or waste, in the sense of material that might be inherently interesting or entertaining but has little relevance to the central purpose. The parallels and echoes and interconnections are remarkably intricate, but Kesey provides adequate and skillful signals to guide the attentive reader. Perhaps his greatest achievement is that at the same time it is so unified and coherent, so rigorously shaped by controlling ideas, it is filled with vivid and memorable characters and events. It engages the reader with a sense of spontaneous life. As in *Cuckoo's Nest,* Kesey has successfully located a middle way between merely reporting life on the one hand and distorting life for the sake of message on the other. Furthermore, although the novel's basic themes are few and ultimately rather simple, they are expressed in a rich diversity of characters, incidents, symbols, and motifs. The range of characters runs from a Yale graduate student to an idiosyncratic Indian prostitute. The range of subject runs from youth drug culture to redneck intolerance. The range of motifs spreads from Hamlet to Captain Marvel. Allusions to literary classics appear side by side with vernacular oral tales. To get so many diverse elements working harmoniously to convey a definite theme is a singular accomplishment. It requires an effort and concentration that Kesey has shown no inclination to undertake again.

The summary and analysis of the preceding sections are necessary for an understanding and appreciation of the novel's aims and methods, but they do not convey the ample texture of humor and irony. This is not a comic novel in the same sense that *Cuckoo's Nest* is, but Floyd Evenwrite's frustrated bumblings, Jenny's crazily conglomerated occult quest, Henry's homely antics and anecdotes, and Joe Ben's irrepressible naive optimism are genuinely funny. There are delightful ironies in the way Draeger's self-assured calculations go awry and in the way Wakonda reacts to Hank's apparent capitulation. And there are thought-provoking ironies in Lee's revenge upon his brother.

Great Notion conveys an impression of antiintellectualism that might offend some readers. On the one hand, Lee is a kind of psychologically disturbed sissy who must learn how to take and throw punches before he can straighten himself out. On the other hand, Draeger has ample psychological composure but is a ruthless manipulator. Moreover,

Floyd's attempts at paper-work and brain-work are portrayed as ridiculous. The values asserted in the novel appear to be exclusively those of animal enjoyment of the outdoors, obstinate physical strength, and folksy common sense. Certainly both *Cuckoo's Nest* and *Great Notion* reflect a strong antirationalism. Kesey does not believe in the simple, precise, predictable world of Jonathan Draeger or Nurse Ratched. One of his principal interests in life and art is the exploration of the mysterious human potential for awareness transcending the rational. But his antirationalism should not be equated with hostility toward intellectual strength. *Great Notion* itself is a singular achievement of intellectual power, and Kesey's academic work demonstrates his intellectual brilliance. Although his novels seem to place undue emphasis on uninhibited sense experience, this may be partly a reaction to the tendencies in contemporary technological society that minimize the value of individual effort, alienate man from the natural world, and too facilely systematize human behavior. Kesey has great respect for ideas; he cannot read a book, see a movie, or observe current events without naturally formulating distinctive insights. Consequently, the antiintellectualism of *Great Notion* is more apparent than real.

So far the novel has not come under attack from feminists the way *Cuckoo's Nest* has. This may simply be because it has not received the critical attention that first novel has. The potential for feminist complaint is probably there. The world of the novel is distinctively a masculine one. Viv's sorrow at having no children is revealed, and the impression is strong that she is not entirely at home at the Stamper house. In the end she leaves in order to find self-fulfillment elsewhere. But despite these attempts to establish her character, she remains little more than a counter or pawn in the conflict between the brothers. We are told near the end that "she has never really understood, not just since Lee came to Oregon, but since she came" (623). And when she does understand she sees how they have all been cheated in this brother-mother-wife-lover tangle. Judging from his notes, Kesey originally intended to do more with Viv, and perhaps her motivations would have been clearer if he had; but it is clear that given the central thrust of the novel, she was destined to play a subsidiary role. That she and other women in the book are of secondary importance, and are portrayed to some extent as pliantly male dominated, might be construed as antifeminism, but to do so questions the author's right to focus his attention rather exclusively upon a masculine context. In reality, the question of the nature and value of genuine strength, although treated largely in male terms in this novel, is made relevant to both sexes. That Viv is not developed fully enough is perhaps a reasonable criticism; but to suggest she is treated unsympathetically or demeaningly would be unreasonable. In an interview with Paul Krassner in 1971, Kesey said, "Women's Lib was the real issue in *Notion*. I didn't know this when I wrote it, but think about it: It's about men matching egos and wills on the battleground of Vivian's unconsulted hide. When she leaves at the end of the book, she chooses to leave the only people she loves for a bleak and uncertain but at least *equal* future."[17]

Some readers find the dangling arm shocking and question the taste of using such a device, and they wonder if the incident is too far-fetched. There is no doubt about the shock effect. Kesey intended it to be arresting and memorable, and here again his notes are useful in revealing just how the idea took shape. He wanted to begin with a sense of urgency in the present tense. He first thought of using a leg, and as he questioned himself about what the leg would signify, he changed his mind. "Perhaps an arm instead, tied around the wrist as the hand seems to be gripping the rope. Holding itself out of the water, the hand gripping as though it would climb out of the water." This conforms with his thinking concerning what the river represents, but his mind continued to explore the functions the arm might serve:

> *So the book is on the surface a long exploration of the arm.* And *why* someone would hang such a symbol of defiance.
> The impression given by the hanging arm is one of defiance because of the house's grim defiance. It would be different if it was on a different house, but from this great stubborn tombstone it is defiant.
> So this because it leads me to tell why the house happens to be built as it is.
> *And everything has to have bearing on that arm's being there.* Everything leads to the hanging of it.
> The knot around the arm could be cut away—the arm wouldn't fall.
> How about the finger? Dast I?[18]

This passage reveals a good deal about the way Kesey worked. It shows how clear the basic conception was in his mind and how firmly committed he was to having all parts contribute to the central incident.

It shows how carefully he pondered symbols and considered their relationship to theme. And it shows his sense of risk. Each reader must decide whether the risk was justified in this particular case. Although the severed arm is gruesome and somewhat bewildering when it appears on the second page, by the end of the novel most readers are willing to believe the Stampers capable of such an act of defiance.

A question that cannot be avoided in an evaluation of the novel is whether or not Kesey went too far in experiments with narrative techniques. Does the law of diminishing returns enter at some point in his piling on of devices? This question is difficult to answer because reader skills and tastes vary greatly, and it is difficult to envision what the novel would be like with fewer of those devices. The general appeal of the book is obviously diminished by its experimental methods. That it is less popular than *Cuckoo's Nest* is not surprising. So from the standpoint of popular appeal Kesey's experiments fail. But from the standpoint of serious artistic endeavor the answer is not so simple. Perhaps there is a certain amount of overkill in his use of multiple techniques in the quest to convey the complexity and full dimensions of reality, but the reader who is willing to give the novel more than one reading will find that none of the techniques is there simply for the sake of novelty or to show off the author's ingenuity. There ought to be a place in literature for those works that make special demands upon the reader. Their merit will ultimately be determined by whether or not the rewards adequately compensate the effort. *Great Notion* stands a good chance of meeting that test.

Chapter Four
Kesey as Lightning Rod
More Electrical Forms

Great Notion is a large and technically ambitious novel, obviously the work of a dedicated writer. That Kesey was strongly committed to writing is manifest by his steady productivity during the six years after graduation from the University of Oregon: two unpublished novels and a preliminary draft of a third, a number of short stories, and two published novels, one of them a giant. He wrote to Babbs before *Cuckoo's Nest* was published that writing was becoming more and more a religion with him and he was convinced he would be doing it all his life. As late as the Lish interview in 1963, he mentioned his intention to spend his life writing. But according to Wolfe, by the time *Great Notion* was published the following year, "Kesey was already talking about how writing was an old-fashioned and artificial form and pointing out, for all who cared to look . . . the bus."[1]

The bus was a 1939 International Harvester converted into a kind of camper and painted in a spontaneous and reckless array of primary colors. The destination sign of the front said "Further," and a sign on the back read "Caution: Weird Load." In the spring of 1964, Kesey and a group that had gathered about him at La Honda calling themselves the Merry Pranksters traveled across country and back in it. The experience was a communal psychedelic version of *On the Road*. The ostensible reason for the trip was to visit the World's Fair and be in New York when *Great Notion* was published. More important reasons were to experiment as a group with drugs and make a movie of the experience as it happened. The bus trip and later escapades of the Pranksters are reported in *The Electric Kool-Aid Acid Test* in Tom Wolfe's distinctive style of New Journalism. According to the Keseys, the book has some factual errors and distortions but accurately captures the spirit and atmosphere of the events.

The purpose of this chapter is not to retell what Wolfe has narrated in his fascinating account, but rather to examine these years during the 1960s when Kesey turned away from writing and attempt to answer such questions as these: Why did he give up writing? What motivated his fascination with drugs? And what were the accomplishments or consequences of his experiments with them?

Kesey's experience as guinea pig at the VA hospital awakened a keen curiosity about the consciousness-altering effects of drugs, particularly LSD. At La Honda he began pursuing that curiosity with like-minded friends. At that time LSD was not illegal. They found that the drug experience could be supplemented or enhanced by various audiovisual aids, ranging from day-glo paint to sophisticated electronic equipment. They also created games and activities designed to produce new awareness and altered perceptions and test the drug's effect upon interpersonal relations and communication. The group expanded and the informal experiments, which were essentially parties, became more public. Eventually they became planned public events, the so-called "acid tests." From these developments came acid rock, light shows, psychedelic posters, mixed-media entertainment, and many elements of the hippie culture. Kesey, with his charismatic personality, became a leader in the psychedelic movement and a counterculture hero.

Wolfe's book expanded and perpetuated his reputation as a pioneer in the youth drug culture. After it was published, Kesey was plagued by visitors at his farm in Oregon, sometimes several hundred in a weekend. Some came expecting to live there; others, like pilgrims, wanted to get stoned at the feet of the master. The fact is that many were disappointed to discover that Kesey was not interested and never had been keenly interested in the usual counterculture values. His drug-taking, unconventional behavior, bizarre clothing, the famous bus trip, the pranks—these were not motivated by exactly the same attitudes that animated counterculture activists or hippie dropouts. Kesey was radicalized to some extent while at Perry Lane, enough to be acutely aware of the sterility of the suburbanized, homogenized, and depersonalized aspects of American society; but his base of criticism was closer to that of Hank than to that of Lee. Consequently, he looked toward an old-fashioned frontier tradition of self-reliant individualism for solutions and not, as did many of his young protégés, toward a thin-blooded intellectualism, radical politics, or withdrawal into youthcult. His drug explorations were more a search for new sources and forms of artistic expression than they were a political or cultural rebellion; they were more a quest for heightened consciousness than an escape from an unsatisfactory society.

Kesey's activities with the Pranksters included much that was self-indulgent, irresponsible, immoral, and illegal, at least in the usual acceptance of these terms. An element of immaturity is apparent in the licentious flouting of convention, the obscenity, and the excesses of unrestrained impulses. There are also elements of self-dramatization and self-deception. But, acknowledging this, one still finds at the core of Kesey's escapades a serious spiritual and aesthetic pursuit, misguided though it might have been. An indication of his serious motives is the amount of money he invested in the various Prankster enterprises; most of the money he had made as a writer went into them. By the end of 1965, according to Faye Kesey's bookkeeping, Intrepid Trips Inc., the name of the enterprises, had spent $103,000.[2] It is doubtful that the author of two successful novels would invest so much time, energy, and money in an endeavor unless he hoped to achieve something significant.

The bus trip and the filming of it accounted for most of the expenditure. He spent $70,000 on the film and color processing for what came to be called "The Movie." His brother had invested some also. Kesey had high hopes for the over thirty hours of color film that comprised "The Movie." Wolfe describes it as "the world's first acid film, taken under conditions of total spontaneity barreling through the heartlands of America, recording all *now, in the moment.*" He says Kesey conceived of it as "a total breakthrough in terms of expression . . . but also something that would amaze and delight many multitudes, a movie that could be shown commercially as well as in the esoteric world of the heads."[3] It should be remembered that acting and filmmaking were Kesey's first loves, the focus of his college study and of a keen and persistent ambition. After he had sold the drama and film rights for *Cuckoo's Nest,* he wrote to Kirk Douglas suggesting not only that he write the screenplay himself, but that he also direct the movie. He claimed that he was probably better equipped to do a movie than to do a book, that he had seen more movies than he had read books, and that he knew more certainly where and why a movie goes wrong than he did with a literary work. "The Movie" was an outlet for his cinematic aspirations, as well as being a kind of acid propaganda; but it was an unwieldy and undisciplined undertaking. The difficulty and tedium of editing so many hours of film were formidable obstacles; and besides this, the people at both ends of the camera had often been "dropping acid" and consequently much of the film is out of focus, improperly exposed, and jerky. Parts of "The Movie" were used in the acid tests and for other purposes, but no successful extended version of it was completed. It remains in storage in Los Angeles.

The drug-oriented Prankster activities enabled Kesey to indulge his theatrical tendencies and his interests in expressive media other than the written word. Drugs were the center of his interest because they produced such dramatic effects upon consciousness and perception; but he supplemented the drug experience with group activities, lights, music, film, costumes, and tricks with electronic equipment. It is as though he were trying to satisfy a hunger awakened by books and film and other conventional stimulators of the imagination. If the conventional media can give so much, there must be ways of generating more.

Kesey was ambitious artistically. He wanted to achieve within existing forms, and he wanted to achieve beyond them. Among his papers is this scribble to himself:

After two successful novels and ten times two successful fantasies I find myself wondering "What to prove next? I've shown the buggers I can write, then shown them I can repeat & better the first showing, now what do I prove?"

The answer seems to be "prove nothing."

"A clever challenge, Chaps, and one, I confess, that stirs the fight in me. Now *anyone* can crank out a nice compact commercial, slide it between covers and vend it as literature, but how many are there capable of advancing absolute proof of *nothing*?"

"Not many, no, not so very many."

"Then, by jingo," slapping his thigh vigorously, "let's *do* it!"

Then Resounding HOW?[4]

The "resounding" is written three times nearly on top of each other; the "how" and question mark are in giant block letters. At the bottom of the page five "how's" are written within a block arrow pointing right.

This may be only a kind of doodling, but it indicates how his mind was working in connection with creative expression.

When Kesey returned from his flight to Mexico, Tom Wolfe asked him if it were true that he intended to give up writing. Kesey answered, "I'd rather be a lightning rod than a seismograph," and he talked about new forms of expression in which he and the audience would be joined in a singular way: "It would be all one experience, with all the senses opened wide, words, music, lights, sounds, touch—*lightning*."[5] He told others during this time that he was finished with writing, and while a fugitive he showed up at a creative-writing class at Stanford and told the students that he wanted to move beyond writing to more "electrical forms."

Lightning as a manifestation of power or inspiration has fascinated Kesey. Perhaps it began in childhood when his imagination was sparked by the way Billy Batson was transformed into Captain Marvel in a flash of lightning and that superhero wore a lightning-bolt emblem on his chest. But it continued beyond childhood, for while at La Honda he made himself a colorful superhero scuba outfit with a K on the chest, and described himself to a friend as Kaptain Kelp. His writing often treats lightning. Arnold, the main character in "Zoo," mentions standing "in front of a mirror during a lightning storm trying to convince my soul to fly from my anchoring body." We have already noted the Captain Marvel motif in *Great Notion*. Kesey told Wolfe about a night in Manzanillo, Mexico, when after taking some acid and throwing the I Ching he went out into an electrical storm. He said "there was lightning everywhere and I pointed to the sky and lightning flashed and all of a sudden I had a second skin, of lightning, electricity, like a suit of electricity, and I knew it was in us to be superheroes and that we could become superheroes or nothing."[6] This same experience has an important place in Kesey's movie script *Over the Border,* which is treated in the following chapter. The logo of his magazine, *Spit in the Ocean,* is a jester with lightning bolts shooting from his forefingers. Apparently Kesey needed a symbol for his search for the transcendent, something to represent his hope that a reservoir of human power and vision could be tapped. It was this search that led him to writing and to drugs and the attempt to go beyond both. His choice of lightning may have had something to do with his grandfather's stories of wild horses making thunder; it certainly was connected with Captain Marvel, his favorite childhood superhero; and, of course, lightning has archetypal association with power and illumination. All of these factors must have contributed to that key experience in Mexico.

Search for the Transcendent

In addition to being a pursuit of new forms of expression or aesthetic hedonism, Kesey's Prankster activities were manifestations—as the lightning symbol suggests—of another kind of search that was essentially spiritual or religious. Wolfe has said that the reason he wrote *The Electric Kool-Aid Acid Test* was because he perceived Kesey's group as "a primary religious group." He explains that all religions start with a small group of disciples "who have an overwhelming experience that is psychological, not neurological—a feeling, an overwhelming *ecstasy* that they have interpreted in a religious way and that they want to enable the rest of the world to have so it can understand the *truth* and the *mystery* that has been discovered."[7] Wolfe treats this religious quality of the Pranksters in his book by comparing them with Joachim Wach's paradigm of how religions are founded: "Following a profound new experience, providing a new illumination of the world, the founder, a highly charismatic person, begins enlisting disciples. These followers become an informally but closely knit association, bound together by the new experience, whose nature the founder has revealed and interpreted. . . . A growing sense of solidarity both binds the members together and differentiates them from any other form of social organization."[8] By interpolating such quotations from Wach into his description of the evolution of the Pranksters, Wolfe persuasively demonstrates what they shared in common with religious mystics of various kinds.

Wolfe is correct in identifying the spiritual motive in Kesey's activities. His temperament is clearly oriented toward curiosity about and faith in some kind of Other World. American Transcendentalism, among the manifestations of the mystic impulse, provides an interesting point of comparison. A number of parallels link Kesey with a tradition in American literature that found its most complete expression in Emerson, Thoreau, and Whitman. Kesey was obsessed with what Emerson calls the secret which every intellectual man quickly learns, that beyond the energy of his possessed and conscious intellect he is capable of a new energy (as of an intellect doubled on itself), by abandonment to the nature of things; that beside his privacy of power on which he can draw, by unlocking, at all risks, his human doors, and suffering the ethereal tides to roll and circulate through him; then he is caught up into the life of the Universe, his speech is thunder, his thought is law, and his words are universally intelligible as the plants and animals.

This passage contains the elements Wolfe refers to so frequently as going with the flow, synchronization, Control, Edge City, Cosmo; and opening doors was Kesey's principal metaphor for the drug experience.

Emerson defined Transcendentalism as Idealism in 1842; Kesey's search was Idealism in 1962. Scrape off the day-glo paint, unplug the amplifiers, stash the dope, and the similarities are more apparent. Kesey shared with the Transcendentalist such attitudes as these: (1) love of nature, with the expectation that nature teaches the most important truths; (2) an eclectic approach to finding knowledge, with conventions and institutions largely ignored or resisted; (3) an impatience with the limitations of language; (4) a confidence in intuitive knowledge and an obsession with a transcendental experience; (5) an attraction to the vernacular hero; (6) a feeling that reform must begin with the self; and (7) a predisposition toward mysticism.

A connection between the high-principled, chaste, self-disciplined New Englanders Emerson and Thoreau and the vulgar, licentious, and undisciplined California Pranksters appears at first unlikely. The differences are obvious and significant. But when Whitman and the Beats are considered as links, the continuity is more evident. Whitman joined the transcendental vision with the vulgar, the physical, and the sexual. He introduced the notion that the Other World can be discovered through immersion in the sensuous rather than by an escape from it. This is what James E. Miller, Jr. calls his "inverted mysticism." The Beats responded to this notion and carried it even further from the New England version. Kesey, with a natural inclination toward Transcendentalism, came under the influence of the Beats just when he was shaping his artistic ambitions. Those who admire New England transcendentalism are likely to consider it unfortunate that Kesey's quest for "otherness" was so strongly influenced by the Whitman-Beat version, which seems to lead to self-destructive excesses. They will recognize the idealism, the search for expanded consciousness, but will distrust the possibility of a chemically induced transcendental experience and probably be repelled by the scatological approach to defying convention and achieving harmony with nature.

The Transcendentalists found ordinary forms of expression inadequate for their vision and consequently tried to stretch the language to suit their purposes. Emerson used an Orphic voice, relying heavily on symbols and figurative language, combining rhapsodic suggestive passages with pithy epigrams. Whitman identified the key to his own method as "suggestiveness," and provided a kind of do-it-yourself poetry kit, leading the reader to the end of the transcendental springboard where he must make the leap on his own. He supplied the hints and a catalogue of images, but the experience he was trying to convey cannot be reduced to discursive logic—it must be directly apprehended. The Transcendentalists' impatience with the limitations of ordinary expression and their desire to get beyond them are forcefully expressed by Thoreau in the conclusion to *Walden:* "I fear chiefly lest my expression may not be *extravagant* enough, may not wander far enough beyond the narrow limits of my daily experience, so as to be adequate to the truth of which I have been convinced. . . . I desire to speak somewhere *without* bounds; like a man in a waking moment, to men in their waking moments; for I am convinced that I cannot exaggerate enough even to lay the foundation of a true expression." Kesey felt strongly the same impulse. It is reflected in the distortion and exaggeration of *Cuckoo's Nest* and in the radical treatment of time and point of view in *Great Notion.* When he turned away from writing to Prankster movies and acid tests, he was trying to communicate "somewhere without bounds," and he indulged in an extravagance and exaggeration Thoreau never dreamed of.

A loose sheet among his letters, probably a page from a letter to Babbs, contains this paragraph: "So my reason for laying off fiction writing is a long way from believing that I have written a couple of good-enough books. I like the books and have faith in them, but for all my faith I see holes; more than you or anyone else I can see the holes. These holes are what interest me now. And the worms that bored them." Those holes are probably the areas in which fictional technique, even stretched by experimentation, was inadequate for achieving what he envisioned. If he had heeded Emerson, he would not have tried to fill those holes by resorting to drugs. Emerson was convinced that a genuine transcendental experience could not be achieved through drugs; but, of course, he did not speak with firsthand authority and most of the drugs that enticed Kesey did not exist in his day.

The Lost Tiller

To what extent did Kesey succeed in being a lightning rod? Did drugs enable him to expand his consciousness and enlarge his imaginative powers? We have a perspective of two decades now from which to consider such questions. The relationship between chemical stimulants and creativity has perennial fascination, and Kesey is a particularly instructive case. His experiments as an intelligent and accomplished literary artist, pursued with such faith and commitment, are bound to tell us much about drugs and creativity.

The tapes in the Kesey Collection provide examples of how the experiments were conducted and what they produced. There are eighteen reels recorded on both sides. They were done over a long period of time in a variety of situations. Some are monologues with Kesey registering his impressions spontaneously; others involve group discussion. They are an extraordinary collection of miscellaneous material: Kesey composing by dictation; Kesey telling about his life; conversations at parties; Kesey reporting drug impressions; Kesey providing spontaneous commentary on TV programs and movies; Prankster games and music; the recorder running, ignored or forgotten; and so on. No attempt was made to identify time, place, or participants. There is a good deal of noise and unintelligible talk. But amid the dross of wasted tape, idle and often unintelligible conversation, and plain nonsense are fascinating sections of autobiography, opinion, and drug-induced impressions.

The impressions are what interest us here. Listening to them, one can understand Kesey's curiosity about drugs. The visions are vivid, surprising, constantly changing, and often funny, at least as Kesey describes them. He has an unusual ability for spontaneous description. Maybe this came through practice, beginning with his participation in the government experiments. Much of it is a verbal gift. Anyone who has tried to describe a dream knows the difficulty involved. Events in dreams do not conform to the logic of events in waking life. Analogy and simile are needed as a bridge to bring the listener closer to what the teller experienced. Kesey produces such figurative comparisons fluently. He also has a flair for dramatization and mimicry. But his spontaneous narrations, while fascinating and often entertaining, are always fragmentary. Never is there an extended and totally coherent story or action. This is the first obvious limitation of drug inspiration: it activates the imagination into frantic image making, but the image making is not patterned or structured beyond fragments. There is also a question about whether the drug supplies any substance or whether it simply stimulates arrangements in what the mind already possesses. Kesey's narrations are engaging, when they are, because he has an active imagination and considerable verbal facility even without the stimulation of drugs. The drug simply removes inhibitions and generates rapid and fluent imaginative action. The phenomenon is simply an intensified version of the way certain people become garrulous and witty after a few drinks. A second limitation of drug inspiration, therefore, is that it depends upon a person's natural degree of imagination and verbal facility.

When asked in 1963 how drugs aided creativity, Kesey replied, "The kaleidoscopic pictures, the geometrics of humanity, that one experiences under, say, mescaline, aren't concealed in the white crystals inside the gelatin capsule. They are always in the mind. In the world. Already. The chemical *allows* the pictures to be seen. To know the world you need to see as many sides of it as possible. And this sometimes means using microscopes, telescopes, spectroscopes, even kaleidoscopes." He added that drugs did not create the lyrical and fantastic descriptions in *Cuckoo's Nest* "anymore than Joyce's *eyeglasses* created *Ulysses.*"[9] This seems inconsistent with his claim that the narrator of *Cuckoo's Nest* came out of the peyote itself, but, as we have noted, that claim was probably an overstated attempt to justify, to himself as much as to anyone else, his drug experiments. And it is interesting that in all of Kesey's attempts to use drugs for artistic ends, the single significant example of alleged inspiration is Bromden. This fact is a telling commentary on the efficacy of drug-induced creative inspiration.

Drugs were for Kesey a means rather than an end, and he reached a point where he realized they were not accomplishing what he desired. When he returned from Mexico, he advocated going beyond acid. This was not a popular notion among the youth drug culture. A young LSD enthusiast pointed out to him that those taking LSD are just beginning to open doors in their minds. Kesey answered, "But once you've been through that door, you can't just keep going through it over and over again."[10] Wolfe reports Kesey telling Owsley, a manufacturer and promoter of LSD, "You find what you came to find when you're on acid and we've got to start doing it without acid; there's no use opening the door and going through it and then always going back out again. We've got to move on to the next step." Owsley insists that it is the drugs that do it: "None of it would have happened without the drugs." "No, it's not the drugs," says Kesey. "In fact, I'm going to start telling everyone to start doing it without the drugs."[11]

The case of Kesey indicates that significant art does not come out of capsules. There is nothing one can smoke, swallow, or inject that will take the place of inherent imaginative power and disciplined effort. Kessey's experiment was not only a failure, judged by tangible artistic production, but it may have destroyed a promising literary career, or at least derailed it during valuable youthful years. Kesey's turning away from writing during the 1960s was probably not entirely a matter of choice. His use of drugs led to trouble with the law, and extended legal entanglements produced pressures and bitterness that sapped his writing ambition. The drug-oriented Prankster activities left him little time for serious writing. And of course the physical effects of the drugs were often debilitating. Sustained writing requires a reasonable amount of mental alertness and physical well being. Drugs exacted a price, part of which was paid for in wasted writing opportunities. Wolfe quotes one of Kesey's letters to Larry McMurtry in which Kesey parodies what the straight world thinks of his flight to Mexico. Kesey describes himself as "this young, handsome, successful, happily-married-three-lovely-children father," once valued as an athlete, once possessor of a large bank account, who is now a fugitive. "What was it that had brought a man so high of promise to so low a state in so short a time? Well, the answer can be found in just one short word, my friends, in just one all-well-used syllable: Dope!"[12] Wolfe describes the letter as wild ironic parody, but it is not simply that. Kesey recognized clearly what his drug era had cost him, and the playfulness in acknowledging it only partly conceals genuine regrets.

In an interview in 1970, he said he was abstaining from drugs: "There are dues." When asked what he had learned from them, he said, "The biggest thing I've learned on dope is that there are forces beyond human understanding that are influencing our lives."[13] This is not much when we consider that he was essentially convinced of this before he ever took drugs. His return to Oregon for life on a farm and close involvement with his family is evidence that he had tested psychedelic drugs thoroughly enough to know their nature and consequences and found them wanting.

The drugs may produce extraordinary inner visions, but to call this "expansion" of consciousness may be an error. Suzanne Labin suggests that "displacement" of consciousness is a more apt word: "Not only do the hallucinatory visions not deepen the intuitions that are available to normal consciousness, but drugs nibble away at the normal mind's capacities."[14] James O. Hoge, explains that the drug experience might heighten sensory capacities, but an irresponsible commitment to un-controlled sensation, drug-induced or not, can lure the mind toward anarchy and diminish its desire and ability to cope with conscious experience. "Certainly when used to excess, hallucinogens isolate the self, precluding any possibility of a sensitive response to reality."[15] They disorient the self from a sense of place in history, separate it from family and social traditions, and destroy its interest in the future.

Kesey explains the debilitating effects of drugs in a 1972 interview, using an incident with STP as a focus. His first use of that drug resulted in a bad period for him. "And I forgot something during that period. I lost a thing we take for granted, something that's been forged over I don't know how many thousands of years of human effort, and it's now in us. But when you're very high for a long time, you forget this thing. All I knew when this high was over was that I'd forgotten it, and it was the most important thing I'd ever known and I'd known it since I was a kid." To counter this sense of loss, he took some acid for the first time in a long time. "I thought maybe I could refind this lost thing, but I couldn't cause it's not in the drug. It's in the way we're brought up. In the way our folks deal with each other. The way our uncles and our dads shot the shit behind the pump house. A way of relating that when its gone, leaves you mighty bleak." About this time he decided to go to England, and there he found himself frequently visiting a church graveyard. "There I began to get a sense of what I was doing in England, what I had gone there for, and what I had lost with that STP. I call it the tiller." He explains that when he and his friends took acid ten years before, they cut off their periphery time sense. By focusing intently on the present, they lost their sense of past and future.

We got so we could do it and be right there, in the present, for long periods of time. . . . Powers are available to you that you couldn't find in the past or in the future. But after a while, being in the present is like being at sea, in a boat, and you've been there a long time, drifting and existing. Then you look over yonder and see a light. You decide it's a drag just sitting there in the ocean, in that boat, and you want to try to head toward the light. So you put up your sails and start to try to head out toward the light, but you find that you've lost something else. The thing that enabled you to steer the ship. The thing that was behind you. So you're sitting in this boat in the present, looking toward the light in the future. When I reached for the tiller behind me, after the STP, I found that it wasn't there anymore. I no longer knew what man was doing cruising along through the world.

In the English graveyard he recovered a sense of continuity; he thought of the human spirit that motivates history. "That spirit is the thing that has stirred man and kept him from cracking up on his foolishness. The thing that got us here and moved us across the country—that spirit is a thing that we flipped off, thinking it wasn't important. But without it, we can't maneuver the vessel we're in."[16]

It is easy to see what Kesey is implying with this story of the lost tiller. His explorations of the frontiers of drug visions led him away from his roots—from his family background and from the values and traditions that really provided the thematic core for each of his novels. Beyond that they threatened that fundamental and all-important sense of cohesion with the human spirit working out its destiny within history.

What is Kesey's present opinion about the relationship of drugs and the creative process? He says he believes one should court the muses anyway one can, but drugs do not work for him anymore. He claims they did at first. Other writers, artists, and musicians have reported a similar experience to him. He thinks that even young people trying psychedelic drugs for the first time are not having the same kind of experience he and his friends had in the 1960s. He does not know why, but suggests it may have been a blessed event reserved for a particular time, or there may have been some kind of reservoir that was drained. Judging by his artistic output during his heavy drug-using years, his claim that the drugs helped at first may be colored by nostalgia for a period that was particularly eventful and adventuresome for him. There is no evidence that drugs contributed in any substantive way in his literary creation aside from intensifying his conviction that reality is complex and has larger boundaries than is often recognized.

About the same time he began searching for the lost tiller, his interest in writing reasserted itself. In 1971 he said, "I feel my personal energies swinging back to writing." And when asked if he had not once believed writing is an old-fashioned and artificial occupation, he answered, "I was counting on the millennium. Now I guess I'm tired of waiting."[17]

Even putting aside the debilitating consequences of drugs, Kesey's attempt to go beyond writing was misguided from the beginning for the simple reason that his gifts are verbal gifts. He loves colorful phrases, anecdotes, parables, yarns, and stories. Part of his affinity for narrative is innate, but another large part of it derives from his family heritage and his exposure to the western oral tale tradition. He thinks in stories, conceptualizes in anecdotes. Wolfe noted that "Kesey's explicit teachings were all cryptic, metaphorical; parables, aphorisms."[18] He thought this was part of the Prankster-acid experiment. In reality it was a manifestation of a literary penchant that suited him more to be a writer than to be an acid guru. If anything is demonstrated by Kesey's attempt to be a lightning rod, it is the primacy of the word. In the beginning was the word: and so also at the end. Kesey tried to get beyond it, but the possibility proved illusory, and the attempt was in a way a betrayal of his highest talents.

Chapter Five
Kesey's Garage Sale

Hot Items

When Kesey was released from the prison farm, he moved to an eighty-acre farm outside of Eugene, in Pleasant Hill across the Williamette River. The house on the farm had burned down, so the red barn was remodeled to accommodate his family. The Pranksters joined him, and for a while the farm was a kind of commune. But eventually he felt the need to do the farming on his own. The group dispersed but the Keseys continued to receive numerous and frequent visitors.

Kesey's Garage Sale, a group project, was published in 1973 by Viking, the publisher of his two novels. This is a miscellaneous collection of writings by and about Kesey. It derives from the Prankster era described in *The Electric Kool-Aid Acid Test* and has the flavor and spirit of that period. After an introduction by Arthur Miller, the book is organized into "5 Hot Items." The first, "Who Flew Over What?" is an essay by Kesey describing his introduction to drugs, his work as an aide at the VA hospital, and the writing of *Cuckoo's Nest.* It is illustrated with Kesey's sketches of the characters done when he was writing the novel. The second item, comprising nearly half of the book, is a screenplay titled *Over the Border,* a fictionalized account of Kesey's flight to Mexico. It is profusely illustrated with drawings by Paul Foster. The third section, "Tools from My Chest," is a collection that first appeared in *The Last Supplement to the Whole Earth Catalog,* which Kesey had edited with Paul Krassner. These are short comments on people, books, and things that Kesey considered significant. Hot Item Number 4 is a miscellaneous collection consisting of some of Kesey's notes while in jail, a short essay on creativity, an interview, a letter from Neal Cassady, and poems by Hugh Romney and Allen Ginsberg. The fifth Item is "An Impolite Interview with Ken Kesey" done by Paul Krassner. Added at the end is a "surprise bonus," an exchange of correspondence between Kesey and Laurence Gonzales of *TriQuarterly*. Much of this material had previously appeared in underground magazines.

The book bears the imprint of 1960s psychedelia, particularly the Prankster brand of it. First of all, there is the element of theatricality and put-on, which begins with the cover, a color picture of Kesey strapped to a table surrounded by the Pranksters dressed in white lab coats and nurse uniforms; Ken Babbs is standing over him applying a suction tube (sketched in) to his stomach. The lettering is done in a psychedelic mixture of vivid colors. The items are introduced with pictures of Babbs in a white lab coat, pointer in hand. He identifies himself as Professor Kenneth Justus Barnes, Head Curator of the Prankster Archives, and introduces each item with a tedious mixture of overblown diction and slang. Second, there are appeals for audience involvement. The reader is invited to color the drawings accompanying *Over the Border* and submit them to a contest; and other offers are extended to submit or request various material. Third, there is a mixture of print, photographs, and drawings reminiscent of mixed-media productions. The drawings, described as "acidophilic artisticizing," are in the style of underground comic books. Fourth, there is an antiestablishment tone and talk of drugs and "the Revolution." The epigraph is "The desire for success insures failure." And finally, there is a large amount of the obscene and scatological.

Most reviewers saw the book as a thrown-together combination of recycled spare parts designed to make money. Some who knew little about Kesey's activities with the Pranksters were puzzled why anyone would be interested in the Prankster Archives anyway. One reviewer compared the effect of the long exposition in *Over the Border* to the classic third-grade book report: "This book told me more about kangaroos than I ever wanted to know." The book is nostalgia of a sort, and it is short-term nostalgia with appeal for a limited audience. Mordecai Richler, the reviewer for the *New York Times Book Review,* sensing the in-group quality of the book, made this perceptive observation: "The more I see of the counter-culture, the more it seems to me an inverted Rotary, with its own tired rituals, glad-handers, oafs and uniforms. The flower-children's rebellion, it seems to me, is not so much an attack on the roots of social injustice, informed by truly subversive ideas, as shaped by self-regard and horseplay."[1] This book is a kind of counterculture document directed to other members of the club, but it is also more than that.

It contains little of inherent artistic merit. Kesey's anecdotes about working in the hospital are skillfully done and generate interest. The screenplay has flashes of genius and some fine comic moments. And some passages in "Tools from My Chest" are memorable. But on the whole, these merits are more than counterbalanced by a considerable amount of dross. The collection was apparently put together rapidly and rather carelessly. Mention is made of late additions and rearrangement of sequence. Nevertheless, *Garage Sale* is important for what it reveals about Kesey's interests and values, his relationship to the 1960s counterculture, and his quest for expanded consciousness. The two poles of his career and personality and the tensions between them are apparent. On the one hand, there are California and the frontiers of the drug culture; on the other, there is his Oregon home with its contrasting values. The book is an important document for pursuing answers to such questions as these: Why did Kesey turn aside from writing novels? What was he seeking in drugs and counterculture activities? What are the results or consequences of that search? *Over the Border* is particularly relevant to such questions, because in it Kesey provides a penetrating evaluation of himself as leader and guru.

Of Revolutions

Richler characterizes Arthur Miller's introduction as "solemn" and "necessarily uneasy."[2] Part of the uneasiness is expressed in the first paragraph: "This is, of course, a chaotic volume, and cynics will easily dispose of it as a transparent attempt to capitalize on twice-published material, plus stuff lying at the bottom of the drawer. Or maybe it is just Kesey offering his broad back for his friends, some alive and some dead, to ride on into the public eye." The solemnity follows as Miller makes comparisons between the revolution of the 1930s and that of the 1950s and 1960s. Miller is trying to make some sense of the book in terms of his own experience. As he analyzes his own youth in the 1930s, he realizes that the commonplace distinction between the revolution of the 1930s and the one Kesey was involved in—a contrast between rationalism and mysticism—is not accurate. He realizes that the revolution he experienced was not simply a matter of rational ideas, for when he caught the Marxist vision, "Life suddenly had a transcendent purpose, to spread this news, to lift consciousness." In other words, that earlier revolution was not without its own kind of religious or mystical ingredient. He sees a number of stylistic similarities between the revolutions, but also two important differences. The first is that the revolutionaries of the 1930s wanted changes that would insure a different and desirable future. In contrast, those of the 1960s "would stop time, money time, production time, and its concomitant futurism. . . . You lived now, lied now, loved now, died now." Dope stops money time, production time, and social time; the present moment is all important. The second is that the 1930s radical never imagined that the world could really explode. Youth of the 1960s grew up with a clear consciousness of that possibility. Miller thinks this is behind the movement's style of antic jokiness.

Miller's comparison of the two revolutions is perceptive and interesting, but it is primarily a political analysis from a liberal perspective. Conservatives are likely to be less enthusiastic than he about the gains of the Age of Aquarius. Moreover, the political perspective in an important sense misses the mark, for although Kesey was involved in a movement with political implications, his interests and objectives were not political. The revolution that concerned him was one of individual consciousness.

A more significant note of uneasiness appears at the end of Miller's introduction: "This book and the mind-set it speaks for posit a destiny of utter truthfulness; by letting it all hang out by means of drugs, prayer, or whatever, the flood of impulses merge into a morally undifferentiated receptivity to life, tropism pure. As though evil were merely a fear of what we have within." This perception transcends any narrowly liberal or conservative viewpoint and penetrates to the moral core of the counterculture and Kesey's involvement in it. Discarding conventions and inhibitions and indulging sensuous whims and appetites provide no genuine escape from evil, for evil is not simply a characteristic of the Combine or the Establishment; it is a property of the human beings who create such systems; and it must be confronted within the individual human heart. Drugs, rock music, clothes and hairstyles, and living in communes can be no substitute for responsible, self-disciplined individual effort to confront reality and achieve self-esteem and a satisfactory relationship with others. Miller senses that in *Garage Sale* Kesey has left the 1960s behind. He is right, but it may also be that Kesey was never actually as much a part of the 1960s movement as is commonly assumed. This seems paradoxical since he was a sort of beacon and hierophant. Sometimes his objectives were shaped by counterculture ideas; sometimes counterculture styles just happened to conform with his objectives; but he always retained fundamental attitudes at variance with those of the counterculture. The limits of his allegiance are manifest in *Garage Sale.*

Inspiration

"Who Flew Over What?" begins with a brief account of how Kesey was introduced to LSD. "Of that experience, and the resulting book," he says, "I have been asked certain questions countless times. Let me answer some of those questions here, hopefully for good." His first answers are brief and direct: "Yes, McMurphy was fictional, inspired by the tragic longing of the real men I worked with on the ward. . . . And yes, I did write the book both on the ward and on drugs, double-checking my material so to speak." Then he launches into a story that constitues most of the essay. It is an incident from his experience as a psychiatric aide. He gives it as an answer to a question not explicitly stated: What is the nature of artistic inspiration? This kind of explaining by anecdote, as noted already, is characteristic of Kesey.

The incident involves a patient named Hammerquist, who had had a breakdown during his doctoral oral exam in psychology at Berkeley. He had suddenly addressed the faculty members interviewing him as "Herr Doctor" and "Your Honor" and had said, "Most Holy Grand Inquisitor, why do you force upon me this chalice of rancid piss?" On the ward the only crazy thing he did was put ketchup in his coffee. Kesey did some research and found in an old treatise on folk remedies the prescription for using tomato juice to remove the skunk smell from a dog sprayed with skunk musk. The acetic acid in the juice neutralizes the active olfactory ingredient in the musk, "one of the mercaptans called *ethanethiol.*" Ketchup could serve as a substitute for tomato juice. Noted in passing was the fact that ethanethiol was also the agent giving human urine its particular smell. Kesey put this information together with Hammerquist's mention of a "chalice of rancid piss" and postulated "Repressed Homosexual Fellatio Fantasy."

On one occasion Hammerquist had requested aspirin for a headache. The nurse in charge had refused because she had no doctor's authorization. Kesey had broken the rules and run to his own locker for aspirin and given them to Hammerquist. A week or so later, while Kesey was on the night shift, Hammerquist suddenly appeared and threatened him with a large Coke bottle, demanding to know why he had given him aspirin; was he trying to sabotage the doctors' efforts? Kesey, thinking quickly, said, "Because, Mr. Hammerquist, I had heard that aspirin sometimes counteracts the effects of the mercaptan ethanethiol." The patient, nonplussed, de-committed himself a week later. Kesey says of his reply: "Inspiration. A rare and unreliable commodity responding to no formula, available by no appointment. About all you can say regarding the migratory habits of Inspiration, is that it seems to frequent some areas more than others, and the areas frequented by this phenomena [*sic*] are the places most rigorously avoided by especially American human beings. We can't expect to come up with the brilliant clutch play until we get in a clutch, and even then we can only hope."

What are we to make of this story? It seems to suggest that inspiration, while unpredictable and unharnessed, is not totally mysterious. At least in some cases, it is a matter of a person's knowledge and experience falling into fortunate combination during a time of risk. For a writer this would mean that as he stretches his imagination and takes risks in what he is trying to do, he increases the chances that what he knows will come together in new and meaningful patterns.

Kesey makes a point of informing us that he was not on drugs when he came up with the right answer for Hammerquist. The last section of the essay turns to the question of what inspired Chief Bromden, when drugs were involved: "if real people and situations inspired the novel's secondary characters, and the longings of these people molded the hero, where then did the narrator come from?" He says he used to claim it was peyote, "because it was after choking down eight of the little cactus plants that I wrote the first three pages." Now he does not think so. He has been notified that a certain spirit is peeved at his taking credit "for

messages coming in, as though the receiver were sending the signal."
The suggestion is that Bromden has an existence of his own not
contingent upon Kesey's imagining him. Kesey half expected the
Indian to come to him in a dream and say, "You availed yourself of the
transmission. If you need something of which to be proud, be proud of
this availability." Instead, the ghost of Lou Costello came to him while
he was on DMT and scolded him for thinking he was dead. "How can I
be dead? I'm the funny little guy, loveable [*sic*], and laughable. Wasn't
I here before any actor came along to play me? You want I should fade
out because some little drip in Tarzana kicks the bucket?" This is a
puzzling answer; and what does it have to do with the Hammerquist
story? Is inspiration under drugs different from inspiration without
them? Exactly where did Bromden come from?

Here is one way to interpret the essay. Inspiration with or without
drugs is essentially the same. There is no information, no original
secrets, within the drug itself. The drug can only enlarge or facilitate an
availability on the part of the writer. The availability consists of
recognizing a type or pattern of character or action that will evoke
significant or universal response in readers (as Lou Costello recognized
the type of the laughable and lovable little guy). The specific character
or action that fulfills the type or pattern will be composed from the
author's particular knowledge and experience. Consequently, the inspired writer is one who experiences those moments of illumination in
which personal knowledge and experience mysteriously combine to
form characters and situations that generate responsive chords within
readers, that seem to fit a space that was waiting for them.

This interpretation may not appear to be entirely consistent with the
essay. For example, Kesey says he had not known an Indian before. But
the inconsistency is more apparent than real and results from Kesey's
eagerness to discover creative value in drugs. We have already noted
that he had indeed been interested in and acquainted, at least in some
degree, with Indians prior to creating Bromden. It is true that drugs
reduce inhibitions and stimulate images and activate the mind in
unusual new ways. These effects are obviously relevant to the creative
process. But this artificial stimulation is problematical and certainly
never satisfied Kesey's highest expectations. The question of how much
availability is generated by drugs is far from being answered

adequately, but Kesey seems to have a tendency to attribute greater availability resulting from drugs than his own experience or that of others actually demonstrates.

Over the Border

Kesey studied filmmaking while in college, spent two summers working in Hollywood, used cinematic devices in his novels, and financed the bus trip movie. Finally, he wrote a screenplay. *Over the Border* is a fictionalized, indeed fantasized, version of his escape to Mexico to avoid prosecution for drug arrests. A version of the actual events is narrated in *The Electric Kool-Aid Acid Test*. The table of contents of *Garage Sale* lists Paul Foster, Kathi Wagner, and Ken Babbs along with Kesey as creators of *Over the Border*. Foster provided the abundant illustrations. Apparently Wagner and Babbs contributed small sections (for example, Babbs wrote the section treating the birth of one of his children) and Kesey wrote the rest. It reflects an influence from Wolfe's book. In creating Devlin Deboree, the counterpart of himself (note the alliterating consonants and the end sounds similar to Ken Kesey), he seems to have used Wolfe's portrayal of him in *Acid Test* along with his own actual experience. The relation between the Animal Friends and Devlin also seems influenced by Wolfe's portrait of the Pranksters' relationship to Kesey. It may not be saying too much to describe *Over the Border* as a screenplay based on *Acid Test*. It is difficult to imagine it being written the way it was without Wolfe's book.

The basic plot is uncomplicated. In the prologue we learn that Deboree, the charismatic leader of the Animal Friends (a group united in promoting the psychedelic drug experience), and Behema have been arrested atop a building in San Francisco for possession of marijuana. Evidence of a suicide is staged as a false scent, and he flees to Mexico. The Animal Friends carry out a planned Fest (acid test) and then set out by car and day-glo painted bus to join him. After a slapstick-comedy trip the group is reunited and establishes itself in communal living in Mexico. One night while on drugs during an electrical storm, Deboree imagines he can control the lightning. He has his friends stop the bus so he can mount a hill and demonstrate. A car full of Mexican police happens by and swerves off the road to avoid the bus. Deboree and his three friends have the situation almost smoothed over when one of the policemen discovers drugs in the bus. Deboree escapes, leaving his friends holding the bag. Eventually he and other friends free those in prison by using a homemade hot-air balloon. Together again, the group plans a Fourth of July beach party, at which Deboree wishes to introduce the group into a new dimension of consciousness. At that event Deboree's son is drowned, due to Deboree's negligence. He refuses to accept guilt on the grounds that his cosmic program is more important than compassion. In a surrealistic council scene, his friends judge him and decide to give him another chance. Time is turned back, the boy is saved, and the group leaves the scene.

The screenplay is overlong and too loose a conglomeration of materials. The puns and the slapstick comic situations are often entertaining, and the quest for transcendence arouses interest, but on the whole it is tedious reading. And the overwhelmingly numerous illustrations are more a distraction than a help. They are crude drawings, often tasteless, and when the print overlaps them reading becomes annoyingly difficult. There is a good deal of profanity, belching, farting, urinating, and so on. Perhaps this is an accurate picture of the let-it-all-hang-out philosophy the Pranksters lived by. When the revolution of the 1960s made a housecleaning of middle-class attitudes and conventions, it did a thorough job. Personal courtesy, respect for the sensibilities of others, modesty, the slightest decorum in language or behavior—these went into the trash can along with hypocrisy, bigotry, and militarism. In any case, *Over the Border* is laden with too much gratuitous grossness.

Although it succeeds only partially as a work of art, this screenplay is fascinating and informative as a document of Kesey's search for new awareness and transcendental experience. In it Kesey unsparingly examines himself in his role as psychedelic guru. He is critical of himself for things he did, and he delineates the appalling consequences to which such actions could lead. Devlin Deboree is not an attractive character. He is unfaithful to a patient and devoted wife; he neglects and deserts his family; he runs out on friends; he is self-centered and paranoid; and he comes close to ridding himself of compassion. *Over the*

Border describes a revolution of consciousness gone sour, idealistic intentions corrupted by the corroding impulses to power and vengeance.

Several features make interpretation of this work difficult. It is long, sprawling, and to a degree inchoate. Moreover, the reader cannot be sure how the cooperative effort of composition was carried out and whether or not that effort was tightly controlled by a unified conception of theme and purpose. The amalgam of actual events and people, Tom Wolfe's description of them, and sheer fantasy create puzzling problems for interpretation, which are complicated by generally unintelligible in-group references. Nevertheless, a central idea is made explicit at the beginning and end, which several patterns obviously function to establish.

The prologue begins with this introduction spoken by "Voice in the Sky": "Once upon a time a young man of American background thought he had discovered the Great Secret, the Skeleton Key to the Cosmos, the Absolute Answer to the Age-Old Question asked by every Wizard and Alchemist and Mystic that ever peered curiously into the Perplexing Heavens, by every Doctor and Scientist and Explorer that ever wondered about the Winding Ways of this world, by every Philosopher and Holyman and Politician that ever listened for the Mysterious Song beneath the beat of the Human Heart . . . the answer to 'What Makes It All Go.' "[3] The "once upon a time" opening and the "thought he had discovered" suggest that what follows is an instructive story of a lesson learned. And the man's "American background" indicates that the lesson relates to the American experience. After a scene of Deboree and Behema on the rooftop looking down upon the police who will arrest them, the Voice continues: "And, like all Wizards and Scientists and Holymen before him who thought they had found the Great Secret, our young American thought that he was close upon the answer to the question that always seems to follow finding the answer to 'What Makes It All Go?'—the answer to that even more intriguing question: 'How Do I Drive It?' " (34–35). The focus of what follows, therefore, is not so much upon what the secret is as upon how it can or should be used. The central question is, What are the psychological effects of possessing power or influence? At the end the Voice tells us, "This was only a demonstration of ways not to fly" (169). The young man of American background has begun to ponder "that third inevitable question: 'How do I get off?' " (168). The screenplay is essentially a treatment of Kesey's disillusionment with trying to be a drug prophet.

When Deboree, the "Neon Prophet," plans to go to Mexico, his lawyer asks him what he will do there. He replies, "I'll rest and meditate and feel the waves of the silent earth and seek after the Way, seek quietly after the Way" (38). His seeking after the Way, as it turns out, is a search for cosmic power, which he intends to display at the Polo Grounds in Golden Gate Park to an audience of invited groups ranging from the Hell's Angels to the Sierra Club. This event will usher in "the New Revolutionary War." The principal guidebook for his search is Nietzsche's *Thus Spake Zarathustra*. He compares himself to Zarathustra going into the mountains "to escape the choking self-pity of civilization" (84). The Zarathustra motif is an important one. It is used to develop the notion that attaining new consciousness involves the temptation to Superman elitism and letting the end justify the means. In a conversation with Undine, Deboree belittles feeling and sentiment, particularly nostalgia. He says psychedelics presuppose various levels of consciousness and some, like nostalgia, are to be left behind. Undine says, "I see now why Houlihan is always calling you the 'psychedelic fascist.'" Deboree explains that the Animals Friends and similar groups are working to become *Übermenschen:* "We are all along on this trip as apprentice supermen" (92).

Deboree goes wrong when he becomes "more interested in Power than Flight," when he turns from a revolution of individual consciousness to social revolution: "This is the generation that is going to free the universe. . . . And we, Animal Friends, are to be one of the weapons of that long-awaited liberation" (123). As he becomes obsessed with the grand cause of liberating the universe, he separates himself more and more from responsible and compassionate relationships with those nearest him. This is a common pattern in revolutionary movements: obsession with the abstractions of a holy cause perverts idealism to the point that friendship, family ties, compassion for real people are subordinated to achieving the glorious goal.

Kesey talks about revolution in one of the interviews in *Garage Sale.* The interviewer is a revolutionary, a member of the White Panther party, who wants to know Kesey's attitude toward political revolution.

What he finds out does not please him, and the interview becomes an argument. Kesey says, "I relate to people, not issues." His idea of revolution is to "focus as much as you can on the positive and you try to make the world better around you as much as you can. So much of the problem has been brought about by liberals trying to do something over there." When asked by the interviewer, "What are you doing that's positive for the revolution?" Kesey answers that yesterday he took a little black boy downtown and bought him a pizza. Later he mentions, "You can always find something to walk around with a protest sign to keep from having to do anything right where you are" (204). The interviewer does not respond well to Kesey's notion of individual liberation: "I'm demanding answers, because I think you have information, and I think people can relate to that. And I think that personal liberation is fine, but it has to be related to liberating everybody on the planet." (This is of course what Deboree had in mind.) Kesey answers, "No, listen, what this country needs is sanity. Individual sanity— individual sanity, and all the rest will come true." "Bullshit," says the interviewer. "You can't do it any other way," Kesey continues, "You work from the heart out, you don't work from the issue down" (205).

These opinions help illuminate the final scene of *Over the Border*. It is introduced with Houlihan flying a red, white, and blue kite on the Fourth of July. The Voice in the Sky identifies it as "The Great American Kite" and says there is something wrong with it. The flaw is the string. "No matter how high the Kite, it cannot be said to be flying in the true sense of the word, as long as it is hooked to the earth." The Voice is being ironic in prescribing how we can be liberated in the way Deboree has in mind. It counsels us to cut "the sentimental and sinister and, worst of all, superfluous Kitestring of Compassion. Throw caution and yourself to the winds and cut it! Overrule the snowjob of centuries: clip the Power Line that your flight needs a heartstring to Mother Earth to keep your front to the respiration of heaven! This line is a lie, a civilized subterfuge to make you believe that a Kite cannot really fly but *must be flown*. And be not deceived by variations and disguises; whatever form the connection takes—whether it is a tender tether spun with the purest flax of mercy, or the braided sinews of blackest ambition—it is the same old Party Line. Break it!" (156–57). This lack of discrimination and distinctions in the pursuit of liberation is the principal error of revolutions, the dehumanizing error that Kesey wishes to expose.

It is Deboree's error. He shows up in this scene "absolutely astonishing in an all-white outfit: white boots, white tights, belt and shirt . . . topped by a white satin cape blowing from his shoulders" (155). Here is the Superman ready to demonstrate his power. He has convinced himself that he can control lightning. When a storm moves in, the Animal Friends play amplified music while he points at lightning bolts, saying there's one for the Frisco Federal Building and wham! for the White House and zap! for the Pentagon. In the intoxication of this "heedless press for power and vengeance" (164), he forgets his son, who has been left in a dangerous spot along the beach. The boy is drowned. As the group stares at him while he holds his dead child, he disclaims responsibility and says, "I mean we all know what has to happen to some eggs if we're going to make an omelet, don't we? Eh? So what's with looking at me like a goddamned jury?" He argues that it is just one of those things and blames it on the corrupt condition of American society: "Big cop factories stacked all over and cattle castles fouling the air till you can't see and crooked, lying insurance salesmen *coax* these calamities!" He plans to continue "swinging and grooving and laughing flowers and powers": "I'm a volunteer for Liberation of the Universe and I don't care how many eggs get cracked. I've got to be hard, you dig? Strong!" (161). The *deus ex machina* of fantasy enters at the end and rolls back time to provide Deboree with another chance and the reader with a happy ending. But the point has been made, and it is emphasized by the Animal Friends mockingly comparing him to Charles Manson. The title refers to more than the Mexican border. There is a border between healthy personal liberation and social/moral anarchy; crossing over it has disastrous consequences.

Lightning plays an important role in this screenplay, as is suggested by the picture on the title page of Reddy Kilowatt with a lightning bolt and the word "Shazam" above his head. We have already considered Kesey's fascination with lightning as a symbol for transforming revelation or power. It should be noted, however, that both in *Great Notion* and *Over the Border* lightning is treated ambivalently. Lee discovers that the obsession with lightning-controlling words like "Shazam" can lead one away from facing life realistically and cultivating satisfactory relationships with others. Deboree's obsession with lightning leads him to the brink of dehumanization. In both cases the fascination with lightning is linked with paranoia. This treatment of the lightning motif may be a clue to Kesey's attitudes, conscious or unconscious, toward attaining the transcendent through drugs. He experienced radical transformations of consciousness and new dimensions of awareness and sensed a potential for an electric creative power; but at the same time, that potential remained forthcoming rather than realized, while the drugs disrupted his life, particularly his family life, and threatened his physical and emotional health.

Tools

The third "Hot Item" of *Garage Sale* is "Tools from My Chest." These short comments on people, books, and things first appeared in *The Last Supplement to the Whole Earth Catalog*. Stewart Brand, editor of *The Whole Earth Catalog,* invited Kesey to guest edit a final supplement. It had been Kesey who had suggested the idea for the *Catalog* to Brand. Kesey agreed to coedit a *Last Supplement* with Paul Krassner, and moved to Palo Alto for two months in the spring of 1971 to do the writing.

In the first entry, he makes clear the spirit of his recommendations. He sees himself as a pointer rather than a seller. Making use of Martin Buber's terms (there is an entry on Buber in which Kesey says, "You can read *I and Thou* in two hours and not get over it for the rest of your life"), he says the pointer should possess the I/Thou consciousness. Sellers are generally employed by the I/It possessers and expect to gain from the selling. He intends just to point out influences that have been significant for him.

Being in Palo Alto again reminds him of the activities he began there ten years before and prompts him to reflect upon the drug experience. He claims that the first drug trips had a cleansing and liberating effect and enabled people to break through an inhibiting shell. But conditions did not change, and people had to reconcile themselves to them. "So, what with justification being the spawning ground of theory and theory being the back-up of justification, it didn't take us long to begin to take on new shells—different shells, to be sure, of dazzling design, but, if anything, more dangerous than our original Middle-class-American Armorplate with its Johnson's glo-coat finish—because drugs, those miracle tools that had first stripped us, were now being included in the manufacturing of our new shell of theories. The old story" (175). This clearly implies a disillusionment with drugs and the drug culture. We might expect Kesey to recognize an element of self-deception in those first trips, but he retains a nostalgic fondness regarding them. But the tools he now recommends are not chemical, with the exception of marijuana; he still recommends "good old grass." What kinds of things does he consider useful tools? The Bible, the I Ching, dogs, Martin Buber, Malcolm X, Hemingway, Faulkner, the Beatles, Jimmy Durante, Woody Guthrie, the Jefferson Airplane (rock group), flowers, ginseng, William Burroughs, Larry McMurtry, City Lights Book Store, Wendell Berry, mantras, Walt Kelly (creator of Pogo), Timothy Leary, Neal Cassady, and so on.

It is an eclectic collection, probably selected with a variety of motives. Some of the items had been of genuine interest and help to him. Some were probably chosen with an eye to the attitudes and fashions of his audience. Some are kisses blown to friends. And some are undoubtedly there just to startle and amuse. Aside from several engaging anecdotes or parables and some well-turned phrases, the items have no distinctive literary merit. They are useful, however, in revealing Kesey's mind and the fuel it runs on.

The Oregon and California poles that have shaped his values and personality, and the tensions between them, are manifest in this miscellaneous collection. Devlin Deboree, now out of the mainstream of the drug and counterculture movements living on a farm in Oregon, is introduced as "our country correspondent," who will provide "that Natural American wisdom found sometimes in our moody men of the soil" (176). This is the downhome Oregon element that appears juxtaposed with the fads and culture heroes of California youthcult. It is a distinctive Kesey blending. A similar characteristic mixture is that of the earthy and the spiritual, a product of the Beats and a frequent attribute in the 1960s revolution. It is a combination of the coarse, slangy, and obscene with spiritual search. To understand Kesey is to understand a man who carries the Bible and *Naked Lunch* in the same toolbox.

A number of the items reflect that search Kesey began as a boy when he received the magic book in the mail with the Batman decals. It is a hungry curiosity for supernatural experience, for enlarging the dimensions of human consciousness. It is basically a religious impulse with a Christian orientation. Indeed, he calls himself a Christian. The item on the Bible contains a personal experience in which he and his son were hit by a train. The boy appeared dead to him, but was revived after he prayed fervently. "What amazed me . . . was that when the chips were down I knew *where* to call, and that I knew Who answered" (176). Yet the impulse is eclectic, as though he wants to cover all bases; so along with the Bible and Christianity he turns to the I Ching, rock music, mantras, or whatever else promises a taste of the transcendent or otherness. For example, he says, "The Bible is, for me, a tool of light and the Ching is [the] most practical day-by-dawdling-day tool of the Way" (177). There may be an element of self-parody in *Great Notion* when he describes Indian Jenny's experimenting with every alleged magic or occult system she learns about. And in a way Kesey's rootless spiritual aspiration is symptomatic of our age. Orthodox Christianity has been so widely discredited in a secularized society that even a person who is tied to it by family tradition and natural inclination cannot rest at anchor in it. And at the same time, the spiritual sterility of much of contemporary American life generates a yearning for spiritual voyaging. The result is that young people turn to drugs, Eastern religions, cults, witchcraft, science fiction and fantasy, or anything else that opens a vista beyond the perplexing realities of the modern world. "Tools from My Chest" documents Kesey's attempts to cope with this modern dilemma.

Miscellaneous

The remainder of *Garage Sale,* Hot Items 4 and 5 and "The Surprise Bonus," is a miscellaneous assortment of previously published items: a few notes Kesey made while in jail; a spoof on exercises in creation; two interviews with Kesey; a poem on Neal Cassady by Hugh Romney; a frenetic letter from Cassady to Kesey; two poems by Allen Ginsberg; and an exchange of letters between Kesey and Laurence Gonzales. This assortment is probably what Arthur Miller had in mind when he mentions "stuff lying at the bottom of the drawer" in his introduction. The jail notes and the interviews are interesting because they reveal Kesey's personality, and he is a fascinating personality. Much of the remaining material is embarrassingly silly and at times rather disgusting.

The jail notes were for a novel Kesey worked on while at the prison farm. He calls it "an illuminated novel," using the terms in the sense of a manuscript decorated with elaborate designs or pictures. It is done on large rectangles of poster board, forty of them, about 18 by 24 inches. These pages are covered with felt pen writing and drawings, clippings from newspapers and magazines, and scraps of handwritten text. Often the lettering is large or specially shaped for emphasis. It is a montage effect ordered by a continuous narrative. The title is "Cut the Motherfuckers Loose." It appears to be mainly direct reporting of his prison experience and contains a good deal of profanity, prison argot, and details of prison routine. But the focus is on the black inmates and the tense relation between them and the white guards and inmates. The manuscript needs reworking and completion before it would be ready for publication, and Kesey has toyed with the idea of completing it. He mentions in the Krassner interview that he is working on a "new totally fictional version" of it. But it probably is a difficult manuscript to revise. It was created out of an intense and unusual experience that cannot be adequately recaptured in retrospect. Moreover, the experience is one he has put behind him and probably has little inclination to revive in memory.

The interviews include opinions that do not correspond with the image of Kesey as counterculture hero and prophet of radical consciousness and consequently reveal the distortion of that image. The Argus interviewer obviously expects Kesey to conform with that image and requests from him pronouncements of instruction and inspiration for the revolutionary cause. When he asks him to speak out so everybody in the world can hear his message, Kesey replies, "You can't talk to everybody in the world. There's nothing I have to say to everybody in the world. . . . I know more about my brother's creamery than I do about the revolution" (206, 207). In explaining his attitude toward revolution, Kesey uses the phrase "don't take up the gauntlet" and quotes the book of Matthew: "Resist not evil." He suggests that it is better to face realistically the way things are than to become obsessed and agitated with the way they ought to be. Militant and unreasonably idealistic reactions to injustices inherent in the human condition can produce more harm than good. Paul Krassner, in his interview, also raises the question of revolution: "Where is your vision of revolution in relation to both Ho Chi Minh and Charles Reich [author of *The Greening of America*]?" Kesey's answer: "Well, I think that either sticking a leg in a pair of bell-bottoms or loading a cannister [*sic*] into an anti-aircraft weapon may or may not be a revolutionary act. This is only known at the center of the man doing the act. And *there* is where the revolution must lie, at the *seat of the act's impetus,* so that finally every action, every thought and prayer, springs from this committed center" (218). Like Emerson and Thoreau, Kesey desires revolution of a kind, but it is a revolution inside the individual. If this is accomplished, corresponding changes in society will follow.

Both interviews reveal a reticence on Kesey's part to make pronouncements on complex issues. As he tells Krassner, "I don't like the sound of me answering too-hard questions" (225). All the same, he acknowledges that he is easily tempted to do so when someone approaches him with a notepad or a microphone. Everyone is. This is one of the dangers of media exposure. One of the more interesting of his responses is a forceful argument against abortion, which he describes as "fascism again, back as a fad in a new intellectual garb with a new, and more helpless, victim" (219). Another is his concept of "the communal lie," which is a criticism of the self-deception involved in commune living. He acknowledges that the entire psychedelic community, himself included, participated in it. Style disguised a lack of substance; being part of a collective became an escape from reality and personal responsibility. "Being beautiful, or cool, or hip is too often a clean-up for not pulling weeds" (220). Woodstock was beautiful, he says, but Altamont was more honest.

There is not much in *Garage Sale* that is built to last. Already some of the hip phrases seem dated, and the people and events alluded to are growing unfamiliar—some were not widely known in the first place. If the book should be remembered at all, which is doubtful, it will be as a record of Kesey's psychedelic era or a document of 1960s radical culture.

Chapter Six
Spit in the Ocean

Further Adventures of Devlin Deboree

The title page of *Garage Sale* announces that the book is a joint production of the Viking Press and Intrepid Trips Information Service. Intrepid Trips was created in the early 1960s at the time of the Prankster bus trip. It is the title for the various enterprises Kesey and his friends have engaged in since that time. The logo, apparently created by Paul Foster, is a drawing of the Statue of Liberty, torch held aloft, riding upon a six-fingered hand that is racing along ahead of a small cloud of dust. The lady's hair and gown are flowing in the wind as she speaks into a cartoon balloon, "Faster!" Within *Garage Sale* is a full-page ad (including subscription coupon) for Intrepid Trips' next enterprise, a magazine called *Spit in the Ocean*.

Spit in the Ocean or SITO, as the jester who appears on each cover is called, was planned for seven issues, each to be guest edited and devoted to a specific theme. And each would contain an installment of Kesey's next novel, *Seven Prayers by Grandma Whittier*. No time schedule was established; they would appear periodically. So far six issues have appeared (1974, 1976, 1977, 1978, 1979, 1981). The first, edited by Kesey, addresses the theme "Old in the Streets," or the subject of aging. The theme of the second, edited by "my," is "Getting There from Here." Dedicated to Saul Alinsky, this issue treats the subject of radical social change. The guest editor for the third is Timothy Leary, who chose the theme "Communication with Higher Intelligence." In the fourth, edited by a woman named Lee Marrs, a group of female contributors responds to the theme "Straight from the Gut." Number five is called "The Pyramid Issue" and contains a series of reports Kesey did for *Rolling Stone* on his 1974 trip to Egypt in search of the Secret Pyramid. Richard Loren of the rock group the Grateful Dead and his wife, Elaine, amateur Egyptologists, are the editors. The sixth is "The

Cassady Issue," edited by Ken Babbs. The magazine has a distinctively underground flavor and includes personalities, styles, subjects, and attitudes from the psychedelic revolution of the 1960s.

Most of what Kesey has published since *Garage Sale* has appeared in SITO. Since *Over the Border* he has continued to use Devlin Deboree in his writing. Deboree is the narrator for three obviously autobiographical stories and the reporter of the "Search for the Secret Pyramid." He is also the grandson of Grandma Whittier, the narrator of the novel in progress. Others from the Prankster circle appear with the same names they were given in *Over the Border*. The name Devlin Deboree is intriguing. It has sound similarities to Ken Kesey, but it obviously suggests "devil" and "debris." The name could be taken to refer to bedeviling rubbish or to one who bedevils rubbish (e.g., one who raises the devil with the debris in American culture). Or it may be an updated version of Carlyle's *Teufelsdröckh* ("devil's dirt"), an earlier seeker of the higher consciousness. In any case, when Kesey began writing again after the psychedelic detour following the two novels, his writing has been strongly autobiographical and Devlin Deboree has consistently been the narrative persona. *Seven Prayers* is the only exception, and since that novel is incomplete it is difficult to determine whether Deboree will have more than the minor role he has in the sections so far published.

Kesey felt *Acid Test* left something unresolved. This prompted him to write about the continuing lives of the people involved. The Deboree stories treat the aftermath of the Prankster era, the consequences of it in the lives of the principal participants. It is an interesting case of literary influence. Kesey's escapades inspired Tom Wolfe to a stunning achievement in the New Journalism, at the center of which is a fascinating semifictionalized character named Ken Kesey. Then Kesey himself takes the cue and continues the story of that quasi-fictional character, changing his name to Devlin Deboree.

The first number of SITO has, in addition to the first prayer of Grandma Whittier, a story by Kesey titled "The Thrice-thrown Tranny-man or Orgy at Palo Alto High School." The theme of the issue is aging, and this story is an interesting treatment of it. In Puerto Vallarta, Mexico, Deboree meets a fifty-year-old American who has just destroyed a third transmission in his new Dodge pulling a twenty-foot motor home from Portland, Oregon. As they are having a drink together, Deboree perceives in a momentary look in the man's eye a sense of fear. He interprets it as not ordinary fear, but fear of "the End of the World." What he means by that, apparently, is an end to the world this man has known. It is a fear of aging and the changes it brings.

One of the changes begins when he cruelly berates his wife for an insignificant oversight. She lashes back at him and within a week leaves him. As she reflects on their life together, she remembers how he had done reckless things, "not thoughtless or careless . . . reckless, like to toss me an open bottle of beer when I was down in the basement, hot and cleaning. What could it hurt? even if I hollered no and dropped it? Nothing much lost. But when I hollered no and caught it, I had more than just a bottle of beer, and it was mine! He'd given it but I'd won it! Why'd he stop being reckless and become careless? I know it wasn't all me. What was it caught his attention so that he turned into wood like a puppet? What stiffened his joint and wrecked all those transmissions?"

This last sentence suggests an additional dimension Kesey has given to the Tranny-man's situation. The story indicates his faith in machines. In fact, he values machines so highly that he expects too much from them (the wrecked transmissions), and his sensitivity to human feelings is correspondingly diminished. He is representative of an American society so hooked on technology that it feels threatened by a resurgence of pre-technology values. He tells his friend Wally, "the one thing these long haired freaks *did not know their goddamn ass about* was their notion about the return to the past being a *good*—'We got it better than any *other people on earth ever had it,* and don't you ever forget it!'"

The snapshots (as Deboree calls them) of the Tranny-man and his wife are set off against an experience Deboree had with his father in the same Mexican town. The Tranny man reminds him of his father in several ways: "Many things: the erect exit; the wink; the brusque John Wayne bravado when he spoke of machinery and mechanics . . . many things." His father was approaching death from a rare form of multiple sclerosis. Deboree persuaded him to accompany him and his brother to Mexico, "hoping, I suppose, to get him to understand not only why I had skipped south after my second grass bust, but why I had been smoking dope in the first place." The father, neither a smoker nor a drinker, had never approved of his drug experiments. Once in the early 1960s when Deboree and his brother were trying to grow psilocybin mushrooms in the brother's creamery, the father had sampled the drug, a large dose that produced a hellish night. In the morning he told his sons, "If you guys try to manufacture and sell that stuff I'll crawl all the way to Washington on my hands and *knees* to get it outlawed!" In a poignant aside, Deboree thinks, "could that have been the beginning of your mysterious malady, daddy? We both always wondered, didn't we—?" After that first bad experience, the father had vowed he would experiment no further: "Not until I'm on my deathbed in a blind alley with my back to the wall." When the three reached Puerto Vallarta, he must have felt he had reached that condition, because he was willing to experiment again. They sniffed nitrous oxide together and had a pleasant experience. When the father went to bed, "He'd seen enough to understand that what we were about wasn't evil and—while letting us know it was not for him, or his hardheaded generation—he was no longer going to crawl to Washington to stop us." He said, "You guys better know what gear you're jamming into, though . . . because if you don't make the shift it could be the End of the Universe as we know it."

Near the end Deboree makes explicit the connection between the two stories: "And that's what I'm getting at about the Tranny-man: he knew it was the end but he wouldn't make the shift. Or couldn't. He'd been too long dragging a U.S. weight behind him to go freewheeling across a foreign beach. Because when the Yankee Doodle dream runs out of highway and the hierarchy of destinations is revoked, when reason is revoked, something equally if *not even more important* must be instituted in our lives . . . or universal anarchy will reign."

The story is obviously propaganda for the psychedelic drug cause and magnifies both the crisis in American consciousness and the saving possibilities of mind-altering drugs. It is intended to further "the Revolution," as Kesey perceived it at the time. But on a more subtle level—perhaps even an unconscious level—it reveals some misgivings about drugs. There is a note of guilt concerning the father's illness and death and a sense of need to justify to the father he loves and admires his drug activities and imprisonment. Kesey staked a lot on his drug experiments: money, reputation, creative energies, family relations, and freedom. His claims regarding the benefits of psychedelic drugs must be evaluated with the natural tendency of self-justification in mind. The hopes must be sifted and winnowed from the realities.

On the Farm

"Abdul and Ebenezer" and "The Day After Superman Died," both published in *Esquire,* are set on the farm. Taken together they reveal a shift in Kesey's interests away from the front lines of cultural revolution toward farming.

"Abdul and Ebenezer" is simple reporting of his experience establishing a herd of cattle. The narrator is Devlin Deboree, who sees the experience as a drama. "Not a neat plot or a parable I can yet put a moral to or coax a clear meaning from but it's a drama nevertheless. . . ." This statement, incidentally, indicates Kesey's penchant for finding lessons and parables in daily experience. He started with eight newborn calves, bought cheap because the owners wanted to milk their cows rather than raise the calves. Two died immediately; the other six survived, one of which was named Ebenezer. "She got her misleading name one communal Christmas before we were into checking such things too closely." She acquires a distinct personality from the narrator's description of her. In fact, the charm and humor of the story derive largely from the humanized descriptions of the animals. It is a drama because the narrator attributes to the cattle human motives and responses that create drama. The events themselves are not unusual, just the typical happenings on a farm with an inexperienced owner. The other principal bovine participants in the drama are a Guernsey bull named Hamburger and an Angus bull named Abdul. Both eventually have to be killed because they have learned to breach fences and get into neighboring herds.

The central impression of the story is pastoral. It is an engagingly told account of an amateur cattleman learning the facts of life and death on a farm. The focus is on the fascinating and unpredictable ways of animals, the cycle of the seasons, weather conditions, and man in direct and continual contact with nature. These things are seen through the eyes of a man experiencing a sense of wonder as he discovers them.

Although the animals are delightfully humanized, the farm experience is not romanticized. It is largely a matter of "blood and mud and sweat and shit," with birth and death colliding in poignant and mysterious ways.

A jarring note comes at the end. The family has spent an entire day struggling in a swamp to help a cow deliver a calf. After sundown the task is completed. A beautiful calf is lying in the moonlight. The terrified young cow is standing beside it, her calm and trust just beginning to return. As Deboree cuts the rope by which they have controlled her, a drunk and rowdy rock band explodes into the farmyard, stampeding the cow right over the hapless calf.

Despite the narrator's disclaimer at the beginning that he could put no moral to the story or coax no clear meaning from it, this ending brings together two elements in illuminating contrast. On the one hand is the tiring, responsible, and compassionate effort to assist birth, an effort in harmony with nature. This effort is nullified, on the other hand, by the careless and irresponsible rock band, a kind of epitome of the counterculture. Their association with death is made explicit in their dog's "barking about how many chickens he could kill given the opportunity." Deboree sends them away and returns to the swamp. The incident manifests the tension between two aspects of Kesey's life. Living on the farm seems to have heightened his awareness of the counterculture's negative qualities. The story demonstrates his gift for registering the parabolic vibrations stimulated by ordinary events.

"The Day After Superman Died" demonstrates the same awareness, but the context is considerably more complex. The superman of the title is Neal Cassady. He is called Houlihan here as he was in *Over the Border*. The story is a fictionalized memoir, a sort of tribute to Cassady. Such a story is alluded to obliquely in *Over the Border* when the Animal Friends in California are in touch with Deboree in Mexico through a kind of mental hookup—the kind of telepathic communication Kesey and the Pranksters fantasized about. Wolfe describes the phenomenon in his book as making contact or achieving synchronization. In this cosmic conversation, Houlihan asks Deboree to suppose it is not Easter 1965 but 1972 and he has been dead a couple of years. Suppose, he continues, "that you are reading an article in *Playboy* about *psychopaths* and you find poor deceased *me* put down as bored nut. Some *Playboy* hack calling your buddy a psychopath and him unable to speak a word in his defense. . . . What would you do to avenge this affront?" Deboree says, "Wait a minute! Aren't you a psychopath?" Houlihan replies, "Joyce was blind in one eye. Would you let James Joyce go down for posterity with 'Here Lies a One-Eyed Man' as his only epitaph? Nothing about his style, his genius, his innovative influence?" Deboree says he will try to remember.[1] "The Day After Superman Died" is obviously Deboree's attempt to fulfill this obligation.

For dramatic purposes the story is set in 1969; Cassady actually died in February 1968. Deboree has received a letter from Larry McMurtry, an old literary friend he first met at a graduate writing seminar at Stanford. They had disagreed about beatniks, politics, ethics, and especially psychedelics but nevertheless developed a fondness for each other. They had continued their arguments through correspondence, McMurtry defending the traditional and Deboree championing the radical. McMurtry's latest letter claimed conservative advances and pointed out counterculture mistakes and setbacks. It ended with the question, "So, What has the Good Old Revolution been doing lately?" Deboree has no satisfactory answer, and this provides the essential framework for the story.

A few days after the arrival of the letter, two "California flower children gone to seed and thorn" show up at the farm. They are hitchhiking back to San Francisco from Woodstock. One of them is an angry and disturbed personality whose breath hisses "out of the jagged mouth like a rotten wind." He persists, against Deboree's objections, in throwing a stick for Deboree's dog. The dog is so addicted to fetching that he goes through wires and thorns and gets cut up. Finally, Deboree has to snatch the stick away and insist that the pair leave.

As they leave, Sandy Pawku, one of the group that was with him in Mexico, arrives. She has driven a rental car in low gear all the way from the airport and has just run over a dog belonging to one of Deboree's neighbors. She describes the puppies sniffing around the dead mother and laughs at the whole situation. She is overweight and uses excessive makeup; has been in jail and gone through periods of alcoholism and drug addiction; has participated in the Love and Jesus movements; and has had an abortion and gone through two divorces. She is a pitiful and disgusting specimen of California psychedelia gone sour. Her purpose in coming, aside from desiring a place where she can make a freeloading rest stop, is to tell him that Houlihan is dead. He was found along a Mexican railroad track, the victim of downers and exposure. When he asks about any last words, she says he was conscious long enough to say, "Sixty-four thousand nine hundred and twenty-eight."

When Sandy drives off to do some shopping, Deboree ponders the news. He is hurt and angry and looking for something to blame. In searching for a target big enough to take his fiery blame, he fixes on California: *"That's* where it comes from, he decides. Like those two weirdo hitchhikers, and Sandy Pawku, and the Oakland hippy chick [who informed Sandy about Houlihan's death] who must have been one of that Oakland bunch of pillheads who lured Houlihan back down to Mexico last month . . . all from California! It all started in California, went haywire in California, and now spreads out from California like a crazy tumor under the hide of the whole continent. Woodstock. Big time. Craziness waxing fat."

As he goes out in the woods to bury a lamb that had died mysteriously a few days previously, he discovers a couple of bedrolls, a pack, and the remains of a fire. He realizes this is where the hitchhikers are camped. He drinks from a bottle of wine he finds there and looks at a copy of *On the Road*. "He's read it three times. Years ago. Before heading off to California. Hoping to sign on in some way, to join that joyous voyage, like thousands of other volunteers inspired by the same book, and its vision, and, of course, its incomparable hero." He hides himself in a thicket to await the return of the hitchhikers and begins searching his memory to discover "who this wondrous Houlihan was, what his frenetic life had meant, stood for, died for. Hoping to stave off the mockery of his hero's senseless death and to buttress himself against those bleak digits (64,928!). . . ." He repeats to himself that this is "the year of the downer."

The memories include the first meeting between the two men and also some incidents involving Lars Dolf (modeled on the poet Philip Whalen). In the years of association that followed, they had become "close comrades in adventure and escapade and revolution (yes, damn it, revolution! as surely as Fidel and Che had been comrades, against the same oppressor and the same tyranny of inertia, in the same guerrilla war that was being fought, as Burroughs put it, in 'the space between our cells')." At the end of these recollections, he remembers how Houlihan had used a trick of filling in spaces in his constant chatter with numbers. These were "nonsense numbers to fill the gaps." The thought occurs to him that at the end Houlihan had lost the thread for good "in terminal nonsense and purposeless, meaningless, numbers of nothing."

He dozes off and is awakened when the hitchhikers return with Sandy Pawku. She passes out in a drunken stupor. One of the hitchhikers asks the other what she had said Houlihan was doing on the railroad track. The answer is that he was counting. This is the hint Deboree has been yearning for. "Houlihan wasn't merely making noise—he was *counting*. He didn't lose it. We didn't lose it. We were all counting." The story ends with a long list of personalities mostly from the 1960s—politicians, entertainers, his relatives, his younger self, comic-strip characters, counterculture heroes—fading in and out of his memory.

The ending is puzzling, but, in a sense, this is not unexpected. Kesey is treating subjects that must have been puzzling for him. The story is strategically set in 1969 because it is a reflection on what was for him the most significant of decades. It is an attempt to evaluate the consequences of that period in which he had been so actively involved. He sees clearly and portrays graphically the waste, decadence, and malignant craziness generated by the California psychedelic movement. His perspective from a farm in Oregon, devoting himself to his family and to establishing a responsible relationship with his environment and community, makes the carelessness, irresponsibility, and self-deception of the movement more glaringly apparent. But at the same time, much of his faith and energy went into that movement and he had had many memorable experiences and friendships. His association with Cassady was especially significant to him. Somehow, in this story, he had to be forceful and honest in his criticism of the revolution and at the same time justify his own efforts and particularly the life of Cassady. Superficially he has accomplished this, but ultimately the ugly consequences of the California revolution overshadow the glimmer of hope suggested by the fact that Cassady had been counting.

The story is carefully and skillfully constructed. The lamb symbolizes an innocence that died in the revolution. The cry of a peacock is used to suggest tension. The hitchhikers and Sandy are carefully equated by their cruelty to dogs and other traits. The way the experience unfolds as an answer to the challenge posed in McMurtry's letter provides a satisfying problem and resolution plot. The flashbacks to the early 1960s are adroitly interpolated. But in the final analysis, the story is an uneasy compromise between those two California and Oregon poles that constitute the orientation of his personality and career. Those in sympathy with the revolution will emphasize the note of hope and justification in the ending; those unsympathetic will find that note unconvincing.

Search for the Secret Pyramid

"Search for the Secret Pyramid," which constitutes the first 124 pages of the fifth issue of *Spit in the Ocean* (1979), first appeared in installments in the rock music newspaper *Rolling Stone* in 1974. It is a fictionalized account of his trip to Egypt in the fall of that year. *Rolling Stone* sponsored the trip on the playful pretext that it was to be an expedition in search of what the mystic Edgar Cayce calls the "Hall of Records." Although the search is a spoof, underlying it is Kesey's genuine wish that such things as secret pyramids could be found. An element of self-parody is evident to anyone familiar with his fascination with things occult or mystical.

Devlin Deboree is the author of these dated dispatches, and the trip begins at his farm in Oregon. The first phase is a drive to San Francisco, where he meets Paul Krassner and buys a four-volume set on Pyramidology. Next stop is Dayton, Ohio, to talk to Enoch of Ohio, a pyramid expert and "famous Astral Traveler," who has visited the Valley of the Kings often in his less corporeal form. From Ohio (Krassner gives up the search there) Deboree drives alone to Kentucky, hoping to enlist Wendell Berry in the expedition, but Wendell is too busy with farming. Then on to Virginia Beach, Virginia, to do some research at Cayce's Association for Research and Enlightenment Library. All he learns there is that hundreds have preceded him in his search for psychic Edgar Cayce's Secret Pyramid, the most noteworthy being a certain Muldoon Greggor, who is presently in Egypt doing research. After a brief stop in New York, he flies with Jack Cherry to Cairo.

In Egypt he does little more than the usual sightseeing. He buys a map from "a local mystic" who claims to have seen the Secret Pyramid in a vision. The local mystic turns out to be Marag, one of the guides at the Great Pyramids, who had already sold him some hash. The attempt to follow the map is simply a terrifying ride with one of Marag's relatives to the usual tourist sites. Muldoon Greggor, instead of being a sophisticated Egyptologist, is "your usual ex–acid head, hair still half long, eyes still half slits of some psychedelic scorcher that made him swear off forever. . . ." Among his credentials are experiments in hypnotism with friends in which they made contact with flying saucers in other galaxies. The closest Deboree comes to mystic discoveries is when, just before returning to the United States, Marag takes him to the top of the Great Pyramid and shows him a trick with hyperventilation.

The search for the Secret Pyramid and the mystical knowledge it contains is, of course, a failure. It was a gimmick to interest *Rolling Stone* readers, many of whom were fascinated with the current fashionable syndrome of the occult, exotic religions, science fiction, fantasy, etc. But Deboree indicates that the search was not a total failure. His friendship with Marag and his visit with Marag's family produce for him an understanding and appreciation of a different people and way of life. The implication is that this kind of knowledge is probably more valuable, more useful to human betterment, than any occult knowledge found in secret pyramids.

This is effective travel writing. Places and people are described vividly, and the experiences are conveyed with engaging fullness and delightful touches of humor. Kesey has obviously used considerable fictional license to shape the report.

As a way of reinforcing the theme of quest for spiritual enlightenment, he repeatedly mentions religious holy days and occult beliefs and practices. If the date of an entry has religious significance for someone, he mentions it: Yom Kippur; Succoth, the First Day of Tabernacles; Birthday of St. Theresa; the day Egyptian farmers are signaled by the Pyramid to celebrate their harvest; Ramadan. As he begins the trip he sees "a brass green meteor cross the sky and break into three pieces. . . . Auspicious." He regularly throws the I Ching, and tarot cards are mentioned. Occasional footnotes explain religious beliefs or customs. This is primarily tongue-in-cheek creation of atmosphere, but it also accurately reflects Kesey's eclectic spiritual interests. Deboree describes his own spiritual attitudes after expressing his aversion to "Jesus freaks," disciples of Hare Krishna, and followers of Eastern gurus. He is not looking for "a course in spiritual dynamic tension" or trying to find God in Egypt.

Being raised a hardshell Baptist and trained a hardnose jock, I consider myself adequately blessed with the good build of belief and still fairly fit yet with faith. Besides, going to the Pyramid to find God strikes me as something of an insult to all the other temples I have visited over the years, an affront to all the holy births and deaths and loves and fears I have knelt before and the millions of micrograms of various sacraments taken and the wild words of spiritual teachers harkened to, like St. Cassady and St. Lao Tze and St. Dorothy who, perhaps best of all, sums it up: "If you can't find God in your own backyard in Kansas you probably can't find him in the Great Pyramid in Egypt, either."

Kesey's religious instinct has found expression in a tolerant, secularized, and undiscriminating syncretism.

The element of spoof in the "Search for the Secret Pyramid" does not belie the fact that its author is a genuine searcher. Because Kesey does not take himself too seriously, he can make fun of his own steadfast, yearning preoccupation with the transcendent. He has tried many avenues and on occasion felt tantalizingly close. This frequent experience with near misses is hinted at when Deboree, in describing one of his fantasies, mentions feeling "an old, cold bubble . . . swelling with the familiar chilly ache of almost-found-treasure undisclosing, of forthcoming feasts uncooking, and promises unconsummating, all for the want of communication." In describing another fantasy that falls short of realization, he speaks of "the old cold that bubbles from within when you find yourself helplessly watching communication—precious communication! on the verge of happening!—being thwarted five blocks short of its goal by the inability to communicate." Despite its playfulness, "Search for the Secret Pyramid" ultimately originates in a serious quest that has shaped Kesey's career.

One of the frustrated fantasies that starts the cold bubbling within Deboree is a dream of doing a spectacular music festival at the Great Pyramid. He imagines a brilliant cluster of international performers participating. Kesey returned to Egypt in 1978 when the Grateful Dead performed a concert at the Pyramid. It was a costly project for the rock group—half a million dollars according to the "Furtherlogue" to "Search for the Secret Pyramid"—but it fulfilled a vision of the Dead's manager, Richard Loren, a "pyramidiot."

Grandma Whittier

The first installment of *Seven Prayers by Grandma Whittier* appeared in *Spit in the Ocean* in 1974, the sixth and latest in 1981, and one more is forthcoming. Kesey has referred to it as "form in transit"; earlier sections might be altered and revised as the novel nears completion. He says the novel is an experiment in the sense that he undertook it without a clear conception of where it would take him. He compares it to walking a tightwire without knowing where the other end is attached, or even if it is securely attached to anything. He has found it an interesting experiment, but he has no desire to do it again.

Mrs. Emerson Thoreau Whittier is Devlin Deboree's grandmother. She is patterned after Kesey's Grandmother Smith, and some of her stories are ones Kesey heard from his forebear. With the exception of a few interruptions—more modulations than interruptions—she is the narrator. The chapters, or prayers, as they are called, usually begin with Grandma addressing the Lord. The first pages are italicized, free-flowing, scantily punctuated prose. Then the italics end and the punctuation becomes more regular as she narrates the events of the preceding day. Each episode, in good serial form, ends with a surprising development to pique the reader's curiosity. Here is her story as far as prayer six.

On her eighty-sixth birthday, which happens to fall on Good Friday, Deboree picks up his grandmother from her apartment and takes her to the farm for a party. He has arranged a music festival he calls a "Worship Fair," involving groups of gospel singers, including Grandma's favorite: the Sounding Brass. One of the groups, the Birds of Prayer, is led by M'kehla, a black who plays a minor role in other Deboree stories. He now goes by the name Montgomery Keller-Brown. With his group is his precocious four-year-old son October, or Toby. Grandma is attracted to the child, and suspecting that his innocence is threatened by a cunningly evil father, is prompted to accompany the Birds of Prayer on their bus as they travel the next day to Los Angeles to perform at the Hollywood Bowl on Easter Sunday. Also on the bus, recovering from a crazy spree at the Worship Fair, is fat and clownish Otis Kone (real name Kohn), who is returning to his home in Los Angeles.

During the trip, Grandma learns that the blue-eyed Toby is not Keller-Brown's son, and the boy's mother has not revealed to her husband who the real father is. There is friction between Keller-Brown and his wife, partly for this reason, but more over the question of custody. Toby has been found by Stanford researchers to be an exceptional child, and Keller-Brown has plans for exploiting his gifted boy. He has already begun using him as a kind of shill in a trick he plays by putting salt between the pages of a Bible so it opens to desired verses. He has such a trick planned for their concert at the Hollywood Bowl. Because of Grandma's influence, Toby spoils the trick and infuriates his father. With the help of Otis, who claims he had been drugged by Keller-Brown at the Worship Fair, Grandma runs away with Toby. This unlikely trio, Grandma disguised in blackface, heads for Arkansas, Grandma's childhood home, where she still owns some mineral rights. They get only as far as Las Vegas. They finagled a military flight which, to their surprise, involves a long layover there. As they are trying to cash in their plane tickets in order to transfer to the train, the Birds of Prayer bus shows up and they narrowly escape Keller-Brown and the authorities he has alerted. They leave by train for Santa Fe, but the bus catches up with them along the way. While the train is stopped and Otis is taken into custody, Grandma and Toby flee on foot into the desert.

While they are hiding in the sagebrush from the local jeep posse recruited to find them, a futuristic off-road vehicle appears and they are beckoned by name to enter. The vehicle belongs to a woman known as Miss Vashti, who operates a desert spa somewhere in southern Colorado called Gilead Springs. Her brother, who owns the property, is Merle Travis, a lead guitarist with a rock group named the Airmen. Grandma and Toby accompany Miss Vashti to the remote Gilead Springs, where they find a throng of naked, mud-covered people taking the cure.

There is no point in attempting detailed interpretation of a novel only six-sevenths completed, but some observations are in order. In creating a chase plot, Kesey is diverging from the pattern of his first two novels, in which the conflict derives from a specific location, the mental hospital and the town of Wakonda, respectively. Chase plots have been popular in movies, and this novel manifests the influence of movies and television. The earlier novels employ allusions to typical movie heroes and situations, particularly those of the western, and *Great Notion* makes use of cinematic techniques; but *Seven Prayers* seems imitative in a less artistically significant way. Instead of an ambitious literary work making use of movie motifs, as is the case with *Great Notion,* here we seem to have a novel imitating, without ulterior motive, some of the tired conventions of popular chase movies. But, until the novel is complete, this impression cannot be fully tested. In any case, *Seven Prayers* lacks the richness of images and motifs used so effectively to create unity and coherence in the earlier novels. Perhaps the travel or pursuit framework is intended to serve that purpose.

Grandma Whittier is a delightful character, full of spunk and self-effacing humor. Although she is a devout Baptist, she is tolerant of her grandson Deboree's unconventional ways and peculiar friends. Her common sense, compassion, and sensitivity to the feelings of others win our sympathy, and she possesses the vernacular charm that is one of Kesey's primary strengths. Through her frequent recollections of family and early life, we receive a full impression of her character. Although she is eighty-six and has lived a full and interesting life, her experience in this novel appears to be a kind of initiation into a profounder knowledge of evil. Near the beginning she says, "I never ran into anybody I didn't think but *was good folks,* you get deep enough down." Her friend warns her that "something will happen someday and you'll find out that there are *some* people who are rotten *all* the way down! 'Then,' she says, 'we'll see how that mushy love-thy-neighbor way of yours holds up.'"[2] This seems to be the situation Kesey wishes to explore: the confrontation of innocence and evil. Grandma is referred to at various times as a saint and an angel, and she takes into her charge a four-year-old child. Keller-Brown displays intimations of appalling evil, and several devil-like characters appear in Las Vegas. Kesey says the original conception was to strip Grandma Whittier of all the props of faith—in her religion, her family, her country—and then try to restore them again. It may be that he is testing his own views of life, probing and assaying his own optimistic faith.

Kesey's plan is eventually to combine *Seven Prayers* and the Devlin Deboree stories into one book titled *The Demon Box*. He feels that some of the themes that appear ambiguously in the stories will then emerge with greater clarity.

Chapter Seven
Influences and Achievement

Influences

Kesey's fiction displays a distinctive blending of American traditions. It is obviously an extension of the Beat movement; it reflects the concerns and attitudes of American Transcendentalism; It has the vernacular flavor of frontier humor and the oral tale tradition; and it manifests the themes and character types of the western. These elements are combined with a great admiration for Faulkner and a keen interest in popular culture from comic books to cowboy movies.

The Beats were by far the most important influence upon Kesey. He discovered them at the most impressionable stage in his development, and the discovery was crucial in determining the course of his life and writing. His letters and notes reveal that he was well acquainted with Beat literature before he wrote his novels, and he had observed the Beat life-style at North Beach while a student at Stanford. Neal Cassady was an important influence, at first as Dean Moriarty in *On the Road* and later as a close friend and companion in escapades that constituted a kind of sequel to Kerouac's novels. Some of those involved in the Prankster activities have mentioned that Cassady was the real energizing force in the group, even though Kesey had the role of nonnavigating guru. Michael Goodwin quotes Kesey as saying that Cassady had a lot to do with his losing interest in writing during the 1960s: "I saw that Cassady did everything a novel does, except he did it better 'cause he was livin' it and not writin' about it.

There are numerous parallels between Kesey and the Beats that demonstrate a continuity of ideas, attitudes, and behavior. His relation to them can be described as a transition from disciple to successor. But this obvious continuity should not be allowed to obscure important differences. He possesses attitudes, values, and objectives fundamentally different from and conflicting with those of the Beats. Some of the differences result from his being from the country rather than the city and possessing strong ties to his family background and region. His basic optimism and faith in individual strength of character, originating in his rural western background, produce a basic mental and moral framework fundamentally different from that of the Beats.

This is clearly manifest in his approach to writing. Beat writers like Kerouac and Burroughs were primarily interested in reporting. Kesey has identified himself as a "parabolist" and not a reporter.[2] Reporting does not get at the kind of truth or knowledge he is interested in. He believes experience must be shaped by the intellect and imagination to a significant degree so that it suggests meaning the way a parable does. Moreover, he never adopted Kerouac's notion of "Spontaneous Prose," a notion that considered revision unnecessary and even debilitating. Malcolm Cowley, who was Kesey's teacher and editor, says of him, "He had his visions, but he didn't have the fatal notion of some Beat writers, that the first hasty account of a vision was a sacred text not to be tampered with. He revised, he made deletions and additions; he was working with readers in mind."[3]

The influence of the Beats contributed to a tension within Kesey. It is part of the Oregon-California polarity in his career. He shared their desire for liberation and their thirst for altered states of consciousness and was tempted by their go-with-the-flow philosophy, but his Baptist and rural western backgrounds have pulled him in another direction.

The parallels between Kesey and American Transcendentalism were treated in Chapter 4, but a few more observations are necessary. These parallels can be accounted for partly by his possessing a temperament or spiritual-intellectual predisposition similar to that of the Transcendentalists. Such people are born every generation. But he was also influenced by the writings of Transcendentalism and particularly by the way those writings were assimilated by the Beats. Whitman glorified the common and spiritualized the flesh; he introduced the notion that the mystical or transcendental experience can be achieved by immersion in sensuous experience rather than by escape from it; and he expressed tolerance for the vulgar and criminal. The Beats took these cues and, lacking the nineteenth-century moral and religious assumptions that underlay even Whitman's pronouncements, carried to extremes the notion that self-fulfillment comes from going with the flow and indulging sensuous appetites and instincts. Kesey's transcendentalism in his psychedelic experimenting was primarily of this go-with-the-flow variety. His novels, however, display more of Thoreau's activist self-reliance—controlling the flow or escaping from it.

The fact is there is a certain confusion within his transcendentalism, a tension corresponding to the Oregon-California polarity in his personality. This confusion originates in the concept of going with the flow. Emerson spoke of "the currents of the Universal Being" flowing through him during the transcendental experience. Thoreau also frequently used such current motions as a fundamental metaphor for the vital spiritual element in the universe. To put oneself in harmony with the flow these men envisioned is to magnify one's higher self and experience divine inspiration. It requires intelligent effort and discipline and is quite a different thing from simply submitting oneself to the flux of experience and giving in to instinct, impulse, and appetite. The Beats generally blurred this distinction, and Kesey, under their influence, was victim of the same confusion. But another part of him—the part deriving from his conservative rural and Baptist background—remained slightly suspicious of the flow, hence the resistance to flow in *Great Notion* and his concern with the lost tiller in evaluating his drug experience.

The pattern of migration of Kesey's ancestors corresponds with the westward movement of the tradition of Southwest humor and frontier oral tales. Both began in the middle southern states and moved into Texas, Oklahoma, through Colorado, and into the Northwest. Kesey's artistic disposition derives to a large extent from this tradition. He was born into it. From his early years he listened to members of his family tell stories rich in colorful expressions, earthy and vivid similes, and comic exaggeration. And in addition to acquiring skill in vernacular storytelling by the unconscious process of growing up amid accomplished yarn spinners, he has taken a conscious interest in such folk traditions as those of the confidence man (often noted for his ribald and off-color remarks); the vernacular hero besting the educated city slicker; the preoccupation with physical strength; employing such stylistic techniques as the use of exaggeration, comic similes, dialect, practical jokes, comic juxtapositions and incongruities; the identification of men with various animals; comic treatment of violence, pain, and danger;

and common-sense observations on civilized conventions. All these elements of the frontier and rural traditions of storytelling function significantly in Kesey's fiction.

Blended with them are elements of the western. Kesey frequently alludes to typical western heroes (the Lone Ranger, the Marlboro Man, John Wayne, etc.) and to typical patterns or situations in westerns (conflicts between cattlemen and sheepmen, ranchers and sodbusters; showdowns and shootouts; the fast-draw gunslinger who constantly must confirm his reputation, etc.). But the western influence reflected in his novels goes much deeper than playful allusions to stereotypic characters and situations. It is manifest in the core values expressed in the novels: the preference for the natural over the civilized; the desire for freedom and independence; the importance of self-sufficient strength and a corresponding disregard of civilized conventions; the style of facing danger, injury, and death with taciturn nonchalance or under-statement; the approach of helping others by maintaining one's own strength and integrity rather than relying on collective action; and the recognition that a certain amount of violence or physical conflict is inevitable for the man committed to independence and self-reliant action. Because these values do not always correspond with those of the counterculture, readers who identify Kesey primarily with psychedelic drugs and youthcult are startled when they encounter these essentially conservative values in the novels, particularly in *Great Notion.*

It is these values that largely make up the Oregon side of Kesey's personality and pull against the California side. And it is the tension between the two that accounts for the distinctive quality of his career, in which nineteenth-century rural western attitudes and values are blended with those of twentieth-century urban radicalism. The blend-ing has not been entirely comfortable or fortunate.

Achievement

Kesey's notoriety as psychedelic prophet and hippie culture hero is dissipating, even though Tom Wolfe's fascinating book continues to be read. But *Cuckoo's Nest* and *Great Notion* will probably provide a more lasting reputation for him. What are the characteristics of his achieve-ment that might insure continued reading of his fiction?

First of all, he provides a fresh and original expression of cherished American traditions and values. Americans perhaps have never been as individualistic, self-reliant, and in tune with nature as our myths and traditions make us out to be; but we certainly praise those qualities in our rhetoric. They bolster our pride and sense of identity. We would consider ourselves much poorer without types like Randle McMurphy, Hank Stamper, and Grandma Whittier. Kesey's themes and characters resonate in that part of us that admires the strengths of the western experience, as coarse and antisocial as they sometimes were. Kesey not only embodies in his fiction the ideals of the western myths and traditions, he is at his best when writing in their vernacular and anecdotal idiom.

His humor is a second important strength. It is seldom contrived or strained, but grows naturally out of the situations and idioms of his characters. And most importantly, it is rarely there simply for its own sake; it usually functions to further a serious artistic purpose. It is not the humor of detached wit, but originates in a tolerant delight in human foibles and a recognition that laughter is the best counterweight for pain and narrow sobriety.

A third strength is the intelligence that shapes and controls Kesey's fiction; and, as has already been noted, idea is adequately balanced with imagination so that the characters and events are not obtrusively theme-ridden. Kesey has a remarkable gift for perceiving lessons from experience, morals in simple events. He employs this gift in making his narrative reverberate with meaning. It is a preacher's gift, and it is not surprising that when asked once what he might have been had he lived in another time and without the option of being a writer, he answered, "I'd have been a preacher."[4] It is this gift Kesey probably has in mind when he refers to himself as a "parabolist" rather than a reporter.

A fourth distinctive achievement is Kesey's forceful distinction between the rational and the human. The strictly rational view does not allow for spontaneity and the uniqueness of individuals, and it denies the mystery of human personality. It is the mysterious spiritual component within persons that is the source of real freedom, creativity, and moral character. The Big Nurses and Jonathan Draegers of the world are enemies to the distinctively human aspects of men and women. Kesey is incorrigibly romantic in his insistence upon man's capacity to transcend rational explanations and limitations of his nature.

Kesey's technical inventiveness constitutes a fifth significant achievement. His manipulation of point of view and experimentation with narrative technique are notable accomplishments, combining a perceptive understanding of previous advancements in technique with original invention. His adaptations of cinematic techniques and his use of popular culture for serious purposes are additional accomplishments significant in originality.

A sixth strength is Kesey's honesty and self-criticism. Even his most sympathetic characters are shown with unattractive traits. McMurphy is criminal and psychotic as well as heroic. Hank is coarse and bigoted as well as admirably strong. Grandma Whittier, with all her compassion and common sense, can still be foolish at times. Perhaps this balance contributes to their being such vivid and memorable personalities. And when Kesey writes about himself, he does so with remarkable candor. *Over the Border* is penetrating self-criticism, and the attempt to justify his psychedelic activities during the 1960s in "The Day After Superman Died" does not ignore the negative consequences of that revolution.

Despite these achievements, there are disturbing qualities in Kesey's career. Perhaps more was lost than gained by his California experience. His return to Oregon suggests such a realization on his part. The drug experiments and the attempt to go beyond writing seem to have been misguided. At the height of his literary creation, they distracted him and dissipated his creative energies. The legal entanglements were unsettling and created debilitating anger and bitterness. It is useless to speculate concerning what direction his career might have taken had he stuck diligently to writing, but even the thought of such speculation is saddening. Some believe Kesey burned himself out and expect to see him produce no more significant fiction. The fact that it is now nearly two decades since *Great Notion* was published gives weight to this opinion. But Kesey scarcely seems burned out. Part of the reason for his lack of literary productivity is that he has many interests. There is a strong element of the promoter in him, and he is fascinated with spectacle and performance. A number of projects of various kinds have occupied his attention and distracted him from writing novels. But, again, it was his California escapades that nurtured him as a promoter.

One of the disturbing aspects of Kesey's personality is that his obvious intelligence is combined with an indiscriminate credulity, an overly tolerant curiosity about anything that promises new awareness or communication with another realm of consciousness. In this he is representative of his age and particularly of the youth revolution in California. The 1960s and 1970s produced a renaissance of credulity. Intellectual respectability was granted to belief in witchcraft, flying saucers, reincarnation, tarot cards, pyramid power, transcendental meditation, parapsychology, etc. This eagerness to believe was probably a reaction to the spiritual aridity of modern technological society, orthodox religion—the traditional focus for spiritual yearning—having been discredited in the eyes of many searchers. Kesey's curiosity about any avenue offering the prospect of new awareness has entangled him in a good deal of nonsense and diffused his creative energies.

Perhaps the attitude that had the most unfortunate consequences for his literary career was the go-with-the-flow notion, inherited largely from the Beats. In fact, the Beat influence in general was a less than fortunate one for Kesey, because at the same time it stimulated him, it drew him away from some of his strengths and roots. Going with the flow can produce a temporary exhilaration, but it leads away from the self-disciplined effort required for producing significant literature. *One Flew Over the Cuckoo's Nest* and *Sometimes a Great Notion* were not produced by going with the flow. In addition to hampering serious literary effort, the go-with-the-flow attitude has contributed to the gratuitous obscenity in some of Kesey's writing and his tendency to equate uninhibited sensual expression in language and behavior with spiritual liberation.

In view of the achievement of *Cuckoo's Nest* and *Great Notion* and the long novelistic quiet that followed them, it is difficult not to feel that Kesey took some wrong turns in his career, that promise went unfulfilled and talent was diverted from its proper course. But judging the way a man makes use of his creative gifts is as hazardous as it is easy. Regardless of what Kesey writes or fails to write in the future, he merits respect and recognition for two remarkable novels; and those who admire these novels and desire more can take heart from the stories and novel in progress that have appeared in recent years.

When asked why he has not written more novels in recent years, Kesey explains that his family has occupied most of his attention. Rearing his children is for him a greater concern than writing. He compares the writing process to juggling—keeping many balls in the air at the same time. This requires extreme concentration. When a child comes in with a bloody nose or other problem that must be attended to, the balls fall to the ground and bounce off in every direction, and it is not easy to gather them up and get them in the air again. But now that his children have reached an age of greater self-suffience, he intends to do more writing. Presently he is planning a novel dealing with fishing in Alaska.

Notes and References

Preface

1. Tony Tanner, *City of Words: American Fiction 1957–1970.* (New York, 1971), p. 392.

Chapter One

1. "Excerpts Recorded from an Informal Address by Mr. Kesey to the Parents at Crystal Springs School in Hillsborough, California, Presented under the Auspices of The Chrysalis West Foundation," *Genesis West* 3, nos. 1–2 (1965):40.
2. Gordon Lish, "What the Hell You Looking in Here for, Daisy Mae? An Interview with Ken Kesey," *Genesis West* 2, no. 5 (1963):27.
3. Ibid., pp. 25–26.
4. *Spit in the Ocean,* no. 1 (1974), p. 105.
5. Linda Gaboriau, "Ken Kesey: Summing up the '60's; Sizing up the '70's," *Crawdaddy,* no. 19 (December 1972), p. 38.
6. "A Big Motherfucker," pp. 16–18, Kesey Collection, University of Oregon Library.
7. *One Flew Over the Cuckoo's Nest* (New York, 1962), p. 8.
8. Gaboriau, "Ken Kesey," p. 37.
9. "Kesey on Literature," *New York Times,* 15 May 1979, Sec. C, p. C6, col. 6.
10. Lish, "What the Hell," p. 28.
11. "Ken Kesey at Stanford," in *Kesey,* ed. Michael Strelow and the staff of the *Northwest Review* (Eugene, Oreg., 1977), p. 2.
12. Lish, "What the Hell," p. 25.
13. *Kesey,* p. 3.
14. "The Perry Lane Papers," *Free You* 2, no. 15 (October 1968):20.
15. Ibid.
16. "Who Flew Over What?" *Kesey's Garage Sale* (New York, 1973), p. 7.
17. *Kesey,* pp. 176–88.
18. A photocopy of this page appears in *Kesey,* p. 176.
19. Lovell, "The Perry Lane Papers," p. 20.

Chapter Two

1. Ruth Sullivan, "Big Mama, Big Papa, and Little Sons in Ken Kesey's *One Flew Over the Cuckoo's Nest," Literature and Psychology* 25 (1975):41–42.

2. *Lex et Scientia* 13, nos. 1–2 (1977):1.

3. *One Flew Over the Cuckoo's Nest,* p. 47. Subsequent page references will appear within parentheses in the text.

4. Hugh F. Lena and Bruce London, "An Introduction to Sociology through Fiction Using Kesey's *One Flew Over the Cuckoo's Nest," Teaching Sociology* 6, no. 2 (1979):123–31.

5. *Kesey's Garage Sale,* p. 7.

6. *One Flew Over the Cuckoo's Nest: Text and Criticism,* ed. John Clark Pratt (New York, 1973), pp. 340–45.

7. Tom Wolfe, *The Electric Kool-Aid Acid Test* (New York, 1968), p. 44.

8. Phone conversation 14 December 1971 reported by E. D. Webber in "Keepin' on the Bounce: A Study of Ken Kesey as a Distinctively American Novelist," p. 144, an unpublished thesis—no date or place—in the Kesey Collection. Cf. *Kesey's Garage Sale,* p. 14.

9. Lish, "What the Hell," p. 19.

10. John W. Hunt, "Flying the Cuckoo's Nest: Kesey's Narrator as Norm," *Lex et Scientia* 13, nos. 1–2 (1977):27.

11. Ibid., p. 32.

12. Lish, "What the Hell," p. 23.

13. "The Artistry of Ken Kesey," Ph.D. Diss., University of Oregon, 1971, p. 29.

14. John W. Hunt, "Introduction," *Lex et Scientia* 13, nos. 1–2 (1977):8.

15. Leslie Horst, "Bitches, Twitches, and Eunuchs: Sex-Role Failure and Caricature," *Lex et Scientia* 13, nos. 1–2 (1977):17.

16. Elizabeth McMahon, "The Big Nurse as Ratchet: Sexism in Kesey's *Cuckoo's Nest," CEA Critic* 37, no. 4 (1975):27.

17. Sullivan, "Big Mama," p. 37.

18. R. M. Olderman, *Beyond the Waste Land: The American Novel in the Nineteen-Sixties* (New Haven, 1972), p. 50.

19. Robert Forrey, "Ken Kesey's Psychopathic Savior: A Rejoinder," *Modern Fiction Studies* 21 (1975):224.

20. Ronald Wallace, *The Last Laugh: Form and Affirmation in the Contemporary American Comic Novel* (Columbia, Mo., 1979), pp. 91–93.

21. Michael M. Boardman, "*One Flew Over the Cuckoo's Nest*: Rhetoric and Vision," *Journal of Narrative Technique* 9 (1979):177.

22. Billingsley, "Artistry," p. 22.

23. Wallace, *Last Laugh,* pp. 90–115.

24. Olderman, *Beyond*, pp. 35–51.

25. Sheldon Sacks, "Clarissa and the Tragic Traditions" in *Studies in Eighteenth-Century Culture*, Vol. 2: *Irrationalism in the Eighteenth Century*, ed. Harold E. Pagliaro (Cleveland: Case Western Reserve University Press, 1972), p. 210.

26. Richard Blessing, "The Moving Target: Ken Kesey's Evolving Hero," *Journal of Popular Culture* 4 (1971):615–27.

27. Billingsley, "Artistry," p. 56.

28. Gerald Graff, *Literature Against Itself* (Chicago: University of Chicago Press, 1979), p. 216.

29. T. G. Sherwood, *"One Flew Over the Cuckoo's Nest* and the Comic Strip," *Critique* 13, no. 1 (1971):99–109.

30. Wolfe, *Electric*, p. 35.

31. Lish, "What the Hell," p. 20.

32. Peter Beidler, "From Rabbits to Men: Self-Reliance in the Cuckoo's Nest," *Lex et Scientia* 13, nos. 1–2 (1977):56.

33. Lish, "What the Hell," 29.

34. Sherwood, "One Flew," p. 109.

35. B. E. Wallis, "Christ in the Cuckoo's Nest: or, the Gospel According to Ken Kesey," *Cithara* 12, no. 1 (1972):58.

Chapter Three

1. *Kesey*, p. 81.

2. Lish, "What the Hell," p. 26.

3. Ibid., p. 23.

4. Billingsley, "Artistry," p. 76.

5. *Kesey*, p. 50.

6. Ibid., p. 79.

7. *Sometimes a Great Notion* (New York, 1964), p. 15. Subsequent page references will appear within parentheses in the text.

8. See *Kesey*, pp. 46–49.

9. Ibid., p. 83.

10. Ibid., p. 57.

11. Lish, "What the Hell," p. 23.

12. See the excerpts in *Kesey*, pp. 45–98.

13. Ibid., p. 53–55.

14. Ibid., p. 76.

15. Ibid.

16. E. D. Webber, "Keepin' on the Bounce," pp. 67–68.

17. *Kesey's Garage Sale*, p. 218.

18. *Kesey*, pp. 51–52.

Chapter Four

1. Wolfe, *Electric,* p. 91.
2. Ibid., p. 122.
3. Ibid.
4. *Kesey,* p. 8.
5. Wolfe, *Electric,* p. 8.
6. Ibid., p. 27. See also p. 290.
7. Chet Flippo, "Tom Wolfe: The 'Rolling Stone' Interview," *Rolling Stone,* 21 August 1980. p. 36.
8. Wolfe, *Electric,* pp. 114–15.
9. Lish, "What the Hell," p. 24.
10. Wolfe, *Electric,* p. 27.
11. Ibid., p. 324.
12. Ibid., p. 4.
13. Dick Gaik, "Inching Back into Action," *Good Times* 3 (5 February 1970):7.
14. S. Labin, *Hippies, Drugs and Promiscuity,* tr. Stephanie Winston (New Rochelle, N.Y.: Arlington House, 1972), p. 239.
15. J. O. Hoge, "Psychedelic Stimulation and the Creative Imagination: The Case of Ken Kesey," *Southern Humanities Review* 6 (1972):385.
16. Gaboriau, "Ken Kesey," pp. 38–39.
17. *Kesey's Garage Sale,* pp. 224, 255.
18. Wolfe, *Electric,* p. 112.

Chapter Five

1. *"Kesey's Garage Sale," New York Times Book Review,* 7 October 1973, p. 6.
2. Ibid.
3. *Kesey's Garage Sale.* Subsequent page references will appear within parentheses in the text.

Chapter Six

1. *Kesey's Garage Sale,* p. 65.
2. *Spit in the Ocean,* no. 1 (1974), p. 110.

Chapter Seven

1. Michael Goodwin, "The Ken Kesey Movie," *Rolling Stone,* 7 March 1970, p. 33.

2. Lish, "What the Hell," p. 20.

3. *Kesey,* p. 3.

4. Letter from Peter S. Beagle to E. D. Webber, 17 May 1971, in Webber, "Keepin' on the Bounce," p. 142.

Selected Bibliography

PRIMARY SOURCES

1. Novels

One Flew Over the Cuckoo's Nest. New York: Viking Press, 1962; Toronto: Macmillan, 1962; London: Methuen & Co., 1963; New York: New American Library (Signet Classics), 1963 (paper); New York: Viking Press (Compass Books), 1964 (paper); London: Calder & Boyar, Ltd., 1972; London: Pan Books (Picador Books), 1973 (paper). See also John Clark Pratt, *One Flew Over the Cuckoo's Nest: Text and Criticism,* in the secondary bibliography.

Sometimes a Great Notion. New York: Viking Press, 1964; Toronto: Macmillan, 1964; New York: Bantam Books, 1965 (paper); London: Methuen & Co., 1966; London: Panther Books, 1967 (paper); New York: Viking Press (Compass Books), 1971 (paper).

Seven Prayers by Grandma Whittier. (In progress.) *Spit in the Ocean,* no. 1 (1974), no. 2 (1976), no. 3 (1977), no. 4 (1978), no. 5 (1979), no. 6 (1981).

2. Stories

"The Thrice-Thrown Tranny-Man or Orgy at Palo Alto High School." *Spit in the Ocean,* no. 1 (1974), pp. 37–54.

"Abdul and Ebenezer." *Esquire,* March 1976, pp. 57–58, 146–49.

"The Day After Superman Died." *Esquire,* October 1979, pp. 43–64.

The Day After Superman Died. Northridge, Calif.: Lord John Press, 1980.

3. Miscellaneous Writings

Kesey. Edited by Michael Strelow. Introductions by Malcolm Cowley and John C. Pratt. Eugene, Oreg.: Northwest Review Books, 1977. Selections from the Kesey Collection including notes for the novels, part of *Seven Prayers,* and a scene from "Zoo."

Kesey's Garage Sale. New York: Viking Press, 1973; New York: Viking Press (Compass Books), 1973 (paper).

"Running Into the Great Wall." *Running,* February 1982, pp. 42–63, 73–78.

"Search for the Secret Pyramid." *Spit in the Ocean,* no. 5 (1979), pp. 8–126.

4. Unpublished Material
"End of Autumn." Novel written 1957–58.
"Zoo." Novel written 1959.
Kesey Collection. University of Oregon Library. Miscellaneous manuscripts, notes, letters, drawings, and tapes.

SECONDARY SOURCES

The following abbreviations are used in the annotations: CN = *One Flew Over the Cuckoo's Nest*; SGN = *Sometimes a Great Notion*, KGS = *Kesey's Garage Sale.*

1. Bibliographies
Bischoff, Joan. "Views and Reviews: An Annotated Bibliography." *Lex et Scientia* 13, nos. 1–2 (1977):93–103. Limited to material concerning CN—the novel, the play, and the film.
Weixlmann, Joseph. "Ken Kesey: A Bibliography." *Western American Literature* 10 (1975):219–31. Most complete.
———. "Selected Bibliography." Pratt (fifth printing, 1976), pp. 559–67. Some additions to his 1975 list, but omits items on SGN and KGS.

2. Books, Articles, and Interviews
Barsness, John A. "Ken Kesey: The Hero in Modern Dress." *Bulletin of the Rocky Mountain Modern Language Association* 23 (1969):27–33; reprinted in Pratt, pp. 419–28. Treats the reemergence of the traditional western American hero in CN and SGN.
Billingsley, Ronald G. "The Artistry of Ken Kesey." Diss. University of Oregon, 1971. General literary analysis of CN and SGN, including the most thorough treatment available of narrative technique in SGN.
Blessing, Richard. "The Moving Target: Ken Kesey's Evolving Hero." *Journal of Popular Culture* 4 (1971):615–27. McMurphy changes from frontier hero, confidence man, and phallic hero to ritualistic father-figure whose sacrifice saves his sons.
Boardman, Michael M. "*One Flew Over the Cuckoo's Nest:* Rhetoric and Vision." *Journal of Narrative Technique* 9 (1979):171–83. Argues persuasively that CN is a tragic action and counters feminist objections to the novel.

Boyers, Robert. "Attitudes toward Sex in American 'High Culture.'"
Annals of the American Academy of Political and Social Science 376
(1968):36–52; part reprinted in Pratt, pp. 535–41. Kesey was seduced
by the notion that uninhibited sexuality produces liberation; nevertheless, CN demonstrates that such a belief is no cure for the world's ills.

Carnes, Bruce. *Ken Kesey.* Boise State University Western Writers Series,
no. 12. Boise, Idaho: Boise State University, 1974. General commentary on CN, SGN, and KGS. Short bibliography.

Foster, John Wilson. "Hustling to Some Purpose: Kesey's *One Flew Over the
Cuckoo's Nest.*" *Western American Literature* 9 (1974):115–29. A combination of religious vision and secular hustling constitutes the strategy
and theme of CN.

Gaboriau, Linda. "Ken Kesey: Summing up the '60's; Sizing up the '70's."
Crawdaddy, no. 19 (December 1972), pp. 31–39. Informative interview in which Kesey talks, among other subjects, about his experience
with drugs.

Hoge, James O. "Psychedelic Stimulation and the Creative Imagination:
The Case of Ken Kesey." *Southern Humanities Review* 6 (1972):381–91.
Kesey's drug-oriented activities negated important enduring values in
art by focusing on sensations of the present moment.

Knapp, James F. "Tangled in the Language of the Past: Ken Kesey and
Cultural Revolution." *Midwest Quarterly* 19 (1978):398–412. Analyzes
the tension in Kesey's life and writing between assertive individualism
and interdependent brotherhood and relates it to the cultural revolution
of the sixties.

Lex et Scientia 13, nos. 1–2 (1977). A special double issue devoted to CN,
with fourteen essays on the novel and three on the play and film.
Contributors from a variety of disciplines.

Lish, Gordon. "What the Hell You Looking in Here for, Daisy Mae? An
Interview with Ken Kesey." *Genesis West* 2, no. 5 (1963):17–29. The
most informative of the interviews in terms of Kesey's writing attitudes
and objectives.

Martin, Terence. "*One Flew Over the Cuckoo's Nest* and the High Cost of
Living." *Modern Fiction Studies* 19 (1973):53–55. Emphasizes the
novel's demonstration of the need for interdependence and the courage
to pay the high cost of a free life.

Mills, Nicolaus. "Ken Kesey and the Politics of Laughter." *Centennial
Review* 16 (1972:82–90. Sees sanity as defined in political terms, and
McMurphy teaches the patients that laughter provides a kind of politi-
cal strength even under adverse conditions.

Olderman, Raymond M. *Beyond the Waste Land: A Study of the American Novel in the Nineteen-Sixties.* New Haven, Conn.: Yale University Press, 1972, pp. 35–51. Interprets CN in terms of Eliot's "The Waste Land," with Bromden as Fisher King and McMurphy as Grail Knight.

Pratt, John Clark, ed. *One Flew Over the Cuckoo's Nest: Text and Criticism.* New York: Viking Press, 1973. The text is supplemented by three sections: "The Author and His Work," including letters and drafts; "Literary Criticism"; and "Analogies and Perspectives," including a section of Dale Wasserman's play, articles on psychiatry, and excerpts from other American authors. Topics for research and discussion and bibliography.

Sherman, W. D. "The Novels of Ken Kesey." *Journal of American Studies* 5 (1971):185 96. Sees CN and SGN as literary metaphors for psychedelic experiences.

Sherwood, Terry G. "*One Flew Over the Cuckoo's Nest* and the Comic Strip." *Critique* 13 (1971):96–109; reprinted in Pratt, pp. 382–96. Kesey's use of comic strip themes and methods results in comic strip oversimplification in CN.

Sullivan, Ruth. "Big Mama, Big Papa, and Little Sons in Ken Kesey's *One Flew Over the Cuckoo's Nest.*" *Literature and Psychology* 25 (1975):33–44. Although critical of psychoanalytic therapy, CN uses the typical Oedipal triangle.

Tanner, Tony. "Edge City." *City of Words: American Fiction 1957–1970.* New York: Harper & Row, 1971, pp. 372–92. Good overview treating CN, SGN, and the significance of the Prankster activities, particularly the go-with-the-flow notion.

Waldmeir, Joseph J. "Two Novelists of the Absurd: Heller and Kesey." *Wisconsin Studies in Contemporary Literature* 5 (1964):192–204. Considers CN "the first truly successful American novel of the absurd since World War II.

Wallace, Ronald. *The Last Laugh: Form and Affirmation in the Contemporary American Comic Novel.* Columbia: University of Missouri Press, 1979, pp. 90–115. Criticisms of CN as sexist and racist view the novel as romance and McMurphy as its hero; in reality it is comedy— conforming with classic patterns—and McMurphy does not ultimately embody the book's comic values.

Wallis, Bruce E. "Christ in the Cuckoo's Nest: Or, the Gospel According to Ken Kesey." *Cithara* 12 (1972):52–58. Kesey's gospel of uninhibited sensuality fails to come to terms with the reality of evil.

Wolfe, Tom. *The Electric Kool-Aid Acid Test.* New York: Farrar, Straus and

Giroux, 1968. Lively narration of Kesey's psychedelic escapades, with a summary of his early life and the inspiration for CN. A significant piece of literature in itself.

Zashin, Eliot M. "Political Theorist and Demiurge: The Rise and Fall of Ken Kesey." *Centennial Review* 17 (1973):199–213. Analyzes the political implications of Kesey's activities as described in *The Electric Kool-Aid Acid Test*.

Index